Overcoming Your Alcohol or Drug Problem

Effective Recovery Strategies SECOND EDITION

Therapist Guide

Dennis C. Daley • G. Alan Marlatt

OXFORD
UNIVERSITY PRESS

2006

OXFORD

UNIVERSITY PRESS

Oxford University Press, Inc., publishes works that further
Oxford University's objective of excellence
in research, scholarship, and education.

Oxford   New York
Auckland   Cape Town   Dar es Salaam   Hong Kong   Karachi
Kuala Lumpur   Madrid   Melbourne   Mexico City   Nairobi
New Delhi   Shanghai   Taipei   Toronto

With offices in
Argentina   Austria   Brazil   Chile   Czech Republic   France   Greece
Guatemala   Hungary   Italy   Japan   Poland   Portugal   Singapore
South Korea   Switzerland   Thailand   Turkey   Ukraine   Vietnam

Published by Oxford University Press, Inc.
198 Madison Avenue, New York, New York 10016

www.oup.com

Oxford is a registered trademark of Oxford University Press

Library of Congress Cataloging-in-Publication Data
Daley, Dennis C.
Overcoming your alcohol or drug problem : effective recovery
strategies : therapist guide / Dennis C. Daley, G. Alan Marlatt. —
2nd ed.
    p. cm. — (Treatments that work)
Includes bibliographical references.
ISBN-13: 978-0-19-530773-3
ISBN 0-19-530773-9
1. Substance abuse. 2. Substance abuse—Treatment—Handbooks,
manuals, etc. 3. Recovering addicts—Counseling of—Handbooks,
manuals, etc.   I. Marlatt, G. Alan. II. Title. III. Series.
HV4998.D35 2006
616.86'06—dc22   2006009991

9 8 7 6 5 4 3 2 1

Printed in the United States of America
on acid-free paper

About Treatments *ThatWork*™

Stunning developments in healthcare have taken place over the past several years, but many of our widely accepted interventions and strategies in mental health and behavioral medicine have been brought into question by research evidence as not only lacking benefit, but perhaps inducing harm. Other strategies have been proven effective using the best current standards of evidence, resulting in broad-based recommendations to make these practices more available to the public. Several recent developments are behind this revolution. First, we have arrived at a much deeper understanding of pathology, both psychological and physical, which has led to the development of new, more precisely targeted interventions. Second, our research methodologies have improved substantially, such that we have reduced threats to internal and external validity, making the outcomes more directly applicable to clinical situations. Third, governments around the world and healthcare systems and policymakers have decided that the quality of care should improve, that it should be evidence-based, and that it is in the public's interest to ensure that this happens (Barlow, 2004; Institute of Medicine, 2001).

Of course, the major stumbling block for clinicians everywhere is the accessibility of newly developed evidence-based psychological interventions. Workshops and books can go only so far in acquainting responsible and conscientious practitioners with the latest behavioral healthcare practices and their applicability to individual patients. This new series, "Treatments *ThatWork*™," is devoted to communicating these exciting new interventions to clinicians on the frontlines of practice.

The manuals and workbooks in this series contain step-by-step detailed procedures for assessing and treating specific problems and diagnoses. But this series also goes beyond the books and manuals by providing ancillary materials that will approximate the supervisory process in assisting practitioners in the implementation of these procedures in their practice.

In our emerging healthcare system, the growing consensus is that evidence-based practice offers the most responsible course of action for the mental health professional. All behavioral healthcare clinicians deeply desire to provide the best possible care for their patients. In this series, our aim is to close the dissemination and information gap and make that possible.

This therapist guide, and the companion workbook for clients, addresses the treatment of substance use and abuse. In the United States alone, this group of disorders costs hundreds of billions of dollars each year in treatment expenditures and lost wages and productivity, and kills 500,000 annually. Street crime, homelessness, and gang violence are directly associated with use and abuse.

During the past 15 years we have developed increasingly effective treatments for substance use and abuse. What all of these treatments have in common is a creative blending of approaches that directly address cognitive variables of habitual use and abuse in the form of attributions and appraisals, as well as physical components and social and interpersonal aspects of abuse maintenance. These programs must be individually tailored and focus, in a comprehensive manner, on the issue of relapse vulnerability. In this, the second edition of Daley and Marlatt's influential and widely utilized treatment program, all of these issues are covered, and covered in an expert fashion based on decades of clinical and research experience. Because the authors are originators of interventions for relapse prevention in the addictions (Marlatt & Gordon, 1985), all clinicians will want to include the latest iterations of these strategies in their treatment programs.

David H. Barlow, Editor-in-Chief,
Treatments *ThatWork*™
Boston, Massachusetts

References

Barlow, D.H. (2004). Psychological treatments. *American Psychologist*, 59, 869–878.

Institute of Medicine. (2001). *Crossing the quality chasm: A new health system for the 21st century*. Washington, DC: National Academy Press.

Marlatt, G.A., & Gordon, J.R. (Eds.). (1985). *Relapse prevention: Maintenance strategies in the treatment of addictive behaviors*. New York: Guilford Press.

Acknowledgments

We wish to thank Judith Gordon, Ph.D., and Natalie Daley, M.S.W., for their helpful critiques of the first edition of this book. Thanks to Antoine Douaihy, M.D., for critique of sections of this current edition. We also wish to thank David Barlow, Ph.D., for his help in the first edition of this book. Thanks to Cindy Hurney for help with many tasks related to this edition, and to Paul Kemp for helping with the references.

Finally, we wish to acknowledge Mariclaire Cloutier, Cristina Wojdylo, and Rosanne Hallowell from Oxford University Press for their help with this book.

Contents

Assessing and Treating Co-occurring Psychiatric Disorders

Relapse Prevention and Progress Measurement

Overview of Substance Use Problems and Assessment

Chapter 1   *Introductory Information for Therapists*

Background Information and Purpose of This Program

This Therapist Guide reviews issues in the assessment and treatment of all types of substance use disorders. It is designed to accompany *Overcoming Your Alcohol or Drug Problem: Effective Recovery Strategies, Workbook*. The information and recovery strategies can be used with clients who abuse or are dependent on alcohol, sedatives, tobacco, cocaine, methamphetamines and other stimulants, heroin and other opioids, cannabis, hallucinogens, and inhalants. The guide provides clinicians with strategies for working with substance use disorders by focusing on specific issues involved in both stopping substance use and changing behaviors or lifestyle aspects that contribute to continued substance abuse. The information presented in this guide and in the accompanying Workbook is derived from empirical, clinical, and self-help literature, as well as the authors' experience developing treatment programs and providing direct clinical services.

There are many different types of substance use problems in terms of severity and adverse effects on the client and family. Therefore, treatment will be more effective if the recovery approach is tailored to the needs and problems of the specific client. No single treatment program fits all clients. A challenge for clinicians is to adapt treatment strategies to the specific problems and issues of a particular client.

This guide discusses professional approaches and attitudes toward individuals with substance use disorders, assessment, psychosocial and pharmacotherapeutic treatment of substance use disorders, and self-help programs. It provides an overview of the recovery and relapse processes. The major thrust of this guide is to provide practical clinical strategies to address the most common issues associated with substance use disorders, including:

- Engaging clients in treatment

- Managing cravings and thoughts of using

- Resisting social pressures to use

- Dealing with family and interpersonal conflicts

- Building a recovery support system

- Managing emotions

- Managing co-existing psychiatric disorders

- Achieving balanced living

- Identifying and managing relapse warning signs and high-risk factors

- Interrupting and learning from a lapse or relapse

- Measuring progress

Intended Audience

The first six chapters of this guide provide a brief and basic overview of causes, symptoms, effects, assessment, psychosocial treatments, and pharmacological treatments of substance use disorders. Experienced therapists who are familiar with this information can skip these chapters and focus on Chapters 7 to 21, which describe the common clinical themes and interventions in treatment. Less experienced therapists or those who do not work primarily with substance use disorders will find that the first six chapters provide a general introduction to understanding these disorders.

The treatment strategies discussed in Chapters 7 to 21 can be used with clients, regardless of the therapist's theoretical or clinical orientation. For example, the chapters on managing cravings, thoughts of using substances, and emotions can be used by the 12-step–oriented counselor as well as by therapists who use a behavioral or cognitive approach to treatment.

Chapters 7 to 21 can be used by any professional who is working with a client with a substance use disorder. Each chapter can be used in one or more treatment sessions. The clinical interventions described in these chapters are all designed to engage the client actively in completing recovery assignments aimed at increasing personal awareness and facilitating positive change.

This guide can be used in brief treatment with the client and therapist as they jointly identify specific change issues to review and address during each session. It can also be used in a longer course of treatment, with the focus of the sessions shifting according to the needs and interest of the client. If a limited number of treatment sessions is used, the sessions can be spread out over time so that the client has time to implement and modify the change strategies learned in the sessions.

Chapters 7 to 21 represent the most common issues faced in changing a substance use problem. Less psychologically threatening material is introduced in the early sessions. For clients who have recently relapsed, the therapist can decide with the client which chapters to review and in what order, based on the specific problems and issues presented by the client. Hence, the guide can be used flexibly, depending on where a particular client is in the recovery process. The clinical issues reviewed in this guide, such as managing emotions, can be revisited by clients as their treatment progresses.

How to Use the Workbook

This Therapist Guide provides a brief summary of issues discussed in the accompanying Workbook for the *Overcoming Your Alcohol or Drug Problem* program. The Workbook provides information on a variety of important substance use and recovery topics and offers interactive recovery assignments aimed at helping the client relate to the material in a personal way. This information can be used to identify target areas of change in the therapy or counseling process. The therapist can then help the client develop the requisite coping skills to facilitate personal or lifestyle changes. The specific issues addressed in the workbook can be adapted for clients in various stages of the change process. For example, clients in early recovery can focus on identifying harmful consequences of substance use and raising their level of motivation to change. Clients in later recovery can focus more attention on relapse prevention.

Clients in individual treatment can be assigned specific sections of the Workbook to work on between treatment sessions. Treatment sessions can be used to explore each section in greater detail. The client's approach to recovery assignments and actual answers often provide rich material for treatment sessions.

Any of the chapters that address recovery issues and strategies (Chapters 7 to 21) can be adapted for use in psychoeducational groups in residential, partial hospital, intensive outpatient, outpatient, or aftercare treatment settings. The recommended format for group treatment conducted in residential settings is as follows:

- Introduce the topic of the session and state why it is an important issue to consider in ongoing recovery.

- Select major points for discussion with group members.

- Instruct the participants on how to complete the worksheets.

- Use participants' answers to elaborate on specific recovery issues and coping strategies.

- If time permits, use behavioral rehearsals to illustrate how to deal with interpersonal issues such as refusing offers to use substances or dealing with family conflict.

Group sessions conducted in partial hospital, outpatient, or aftercare settings can use this format with a "check-in" period of 10 to 20 minutes preceding the discussion, in which participants report their last day of substance use and briefly discuss strong cravings, close calls, or actual lapses or relapses. Sessions can end with a "check-out" period in which each client briefly states his or her plan for continued recovery. A major challenge for clinicians conducting topic-oriented recovery groups is to keep the group on the topic and persuade the clients to personally relate to the issues discussed to make the discussion more meaningful for them. Another challenge is to prevent one or two members from dominating the discussions or using the group solely to discuss their personal problems. Because psychoeducational groups aim to provide information and help participants develop coping skills, the group facilitator should ensure that the group holds to the topic unless the circumstances dictate otherwise. The group leader also needs to balance the discussion between problems or recovery challenges and coping strategies. Otherwise, groups will spend all or most of the time talking about problems and struggles, leaving little time to discuss what they can do to cope with these.

Structured psychoeducational group sessions can vary in length from 1 to 2 hours. In outpatient and aftercare settings, additional time is needed for clients to report on their progress and plans for ongoing recovery. Small groups of 6 to 12 clients provide a better opportunity for interaction among group members and personal discussion of recovery issues. The specific topics of the group sessions can be adapted as lectures for large groups of clients. The limitations of lectures to large groups of clients are little, if any, opportunity to make the group an interactive experience and lack of adequate time for participants to complete the written exercises in which they personally relate to the material.

The Workbook is structured to present engagement and early recovery issues before middle and late recovery and maintenance issues. However, because recovery is not a linear process, the therapist can explore whichever issues are relevant to a client at a particular time. Also, many early recovery issues may be revisited later in treatment. For example, a client with 9 months of recovery may suddenly experience a significant increase in cravings for alcohol that are intense and worrisome, or new social pressures to use drugs that lead to increased thoughts of using. The therapist would need to bring these issues to the front of the treatment agenda to reduce the likelihood of relapse.

Need for Additional Psychotherapy or Other Services

Many clients with substance use disorders have other psychiatric, psychological, interpersonal, or vocational problems that require psychotherapy or other types of specialized counseling. These include, but are not limited to, mood disorders, anxiety disorders, psychotic disorders, eating disorders, personality disorders, marital and family problems, interpersonal deficits, lack of vocational skills, inability to find or keep a job, or other life problems. In many instances, once the client establishes a reasonable degree of stability regarding the substance use disorder, he or she is more ready to focus on other types of problems. Chapters 16 and 17 discuss strategies to address co-existing psychiatric disorders.

Therapists or counselors trained in psychotherapy can integrate additional interventions into their work with clients to address other difficulties. However, therapists or counselors who are comfortable focusing solely on substance use disorders will need a network of professionals to whom they can refer the client for help with other problems. In such cases, collaboration is needed to ensure that all professionals involved are working in an integrated fashion.

Other services, such as vocational assessment and counseling, may be needed to help in the client's long-term recovery. Therapists and counselors must use caution to avoid premature referral for vocational training for clients who have more severe types of substance use disorders and are unable to establish continuous and stable recovery. The client without stable recovery who is referred for vocational training is at risk for early dropout, leading to another "failure" experience. Additionally, this leads to poor use of the limited funds available for vocational services.

Essential Skills for the Therapist

Effective clinical work with substance use problems requires versatility and flexibility. Content knowledge and clinical skills in the following areas are needed for the therapist to be effective with clients who have substance use disorders:

- Assessing substance use, effects on the client, motivation to change, coping strategies, and relapse potential

- Assessing the impact of substance use disorder on the family, and addressing family issues and needs if appropriate

- Developing a therapeutic alliance

- Enhancing motivation to examine substance use and to change

- Providing direct treatment by addressing specific recovery issues and problems

- Facilitating linkage between levels of care

- Monitoring change in substance use patterns and related behaviors

- Assessing for psychiatric disorders and ensuring that the client receives treatment for any psychiatric illness

- Collaborating with other service providers

- Making referrals for other needed services (e.g., medical, vocational, psychological, housing, economic, rehabilitation)

- Providing linkage to self-help programs and other treatment programs

- Advocating on behalf of a client

Chapter 2 | *Understanding Substance Use Problems*

(Corresponds to chapters 1 to 3 of the workbook)

Introduction

This chapter provides a brief overview of substance use disorders so that the reader will be familiar with current trends in substance use, the importance of a positive attitude in developing a therapeutic alliance with clients, causes of substance use disorders, the *Diagnostic and Statistical Manual of Mental Disorders, Fourth Edition, Text Revision* (*DSM-IV-TR*; American Psychiatric Association, 2000a) classification of substance-related disorders, specific *DSM-IV-TR* symptoms of dependence and abuse, and problems associated with substance use disorders. The reader who wishes to learn more on any of these topics can consult the References and Suggested Readings.

Definition of Substance Use Problems

A substance use problem exists when the client experiences any type of problem related to the ingestion of alcohol, tobacco, or other drugs, including illicit street drugs and prescribed drugs such as painkillers or tranquilizers. These problems can be in any area of the client's functioning: medical or physical, psychological, family, interpersonal, social, academic, occupational, legal, financial, or spiritual.

Substance abuse and dependence are clinical diagnoses used when the problematic use of substances meets specific *DSM-IV-TR* criteria. Although any type of compound can be abused or can cause physical or psychological addiction, the most commonly abused substances are alcohol, tobacco, and marijuana.

Types of Substances Used and Current Trends

The Epidemiologic Catchment Area (ECA) study, conducted in the 1980s by the National Institute of Health (Robins & Regier, 1991), found that 13.7% of adults in the United States met current or lifetime criteria for alcohol abuse or dependence, and 6.1% met criteria for drug abuse or dependence. Of all the psychiatric and substance disorders studied in adults, alcohol use disorders were the most common and drug use disorders were the third most common.

The majority of smokers in the United States are dependent on tobacco. Unfortunately, tobacco problems are often totally ignored, despite the fact that tobacco dependence is associated with numerous medical problems and fatal diseases and has the highest mortality rate of all substance dependence disorders.

Although there is a trend toward reduced use of certain substances, data clearly indicate that many people have problems with alcohol, tobacco, and other drugs. Even though new trends emerge every several years (e.g., the increase in crack cocaine use in the 1990s, the use of methamphetamine and prescription opiate addiction in recent years), alcohol remains the number-one mind-altering drug abused in the United States and continues to wreak havoc with the lives of many individuals and families.

Attitudes of Professionals and Therapeutic Alliance

Although knowledge and skill are important in clinical work with substance use disorders, the therapist's attitude plays a crucial role in treatment effectiveness. Unhelpful attitudes include cynicism and negativity, lack of hope for recovery, indifference, boredom, a judgmental outlook, rigid adherence to one approach to recovery, and a great need to control the client. Helpful attitudes include hope and optimism for recovery, empathy, lack of anger or hostility, and flexibility in the approach to recovery. Although empathy for clients may be enhanced by the therapist's own experiences in personal recovery, there is no significant difference in effectiveness between therapists who are in recovery and those who are not. Outcome is more influenced by the ability to form a working alliance than the therapist's recovery status.

Helpful attitudes contribute to a therapeutic alliance, a "connection" with the client that is experienced as genuine and helpful. A therapeutic alliance is facilitated when the client feels understood, accepted, liked, and respected by the therapist and develops trust. Treatment outcome is better when there is an alliance with the client. Therefore, the therapist's ability to establish and maintain a therapeutic alliance is a significant variable in treatment outcome.

Substance Use Disorders and Co-occurring Psychiatric Disorders

A recent report by the Center for Substance Abuse Treatment (CSAT) on treating clients with co-occurring substance use and psychiatric disorders presented guidelines for developing a successful therapeutic relationship with these clients. According to CSAT, these guidelines include (2005c, p. 102):

- Develop and use a therapeutic alliance to engage the client in treatment.

- Maintain a recovery perspective.

- Manage countertransference.

- Monitor psychiatric symptoms.

- Use supportive and empathic counseling.

- Employ culturally appropriate methods.

- Increase structure and support.

Causes of Substance Use Problems

Substance use disorders are caused by a number of different factors that vary from one person to the next. These include biological, psychological, and social or environmental factors (Cloninger, 1987, 2005; Gardner, 2005; Higgins & Hil, 2004; Hill et al., 1999, 2001; Leshner, 1998; Lin & Anthenelli, 2005; Martin et al., 1994; McLellan et al., 2000; Moss et al., 1995; O'Brien et al., 1998; Volkow & Fowler, 2000; Wise, 1998).

Biological Factors

Problems with alcohol use disorders in particular run in families, so it is thought that some individuals have a genetic predisposition to develop a problem with alcohol use. It is believed that differences in brain chemistry and metabolism increase the likelihood of developing a substance use disorder. Some people, for example, quickly develop a tolerance for alcohol or other drugs. Their bodies seem to "need" or "want" substances in a way that differs from the bodies of people who do not develop a substance use problem. In addition, some people experience a positive physical effect from substances so that they are "reinforced" each time they ingest the substances.

Psychological Factors

Substances are used to reduce anxiety or tension, to relax, to cope with other unpleasant feelings, or to escape. For some people, this contributes to substance abuse or dependency as they become more accustomed to using alcohol or other drugs to feel better. Others have personality traits that make them more prone to using and subsequently abusing substances.

Social or Environmental Factors

The family and social environment in which people live influences their behavior, including substance use. A person's decision to use or not to use is affected by access to substances, pressure from peers to use, reinforcement from peers for using, observation of role models (e.g., parents) using substances, and standards or values learned from the community or broader culture.

Multiple Factors

A combination of factors can cause a person to develop a substance use disorder. In cases of dependency, the factors that contributed to a person's initial use may differ from those that cause continued use. With some people the physical effects of substances may contribute primarily to their use, whereas with others psychological or social factors may be the primary causes.

Types of Substances Used

Any substance can be part of an abuse or dependency diagnosis or cause problems for the user, even if clinical criteria are not met. Alcohol and tobacco are the most commonly abused substances, followed by marijuana, cocaine and other stimulants, opiates, hallucinogens, and inhalants. Many people use or abuse a variety of substances. Although some people prefer a particular substance or type of substance, others are less discriminating and use many substances.

Classification of Substance Use Disorders

DSM-IV-TR (APA, 2000a) includes several classifications of substance-related disorders:

- *Intoxication* refers to the acute effects of excessive amounts of alcohol or drugs.

- *Withdrawal* refers to a specific syndrome that develops following cessation or reduction of regular and heavy use of a substance (see Chapter 6 for a review of substance-specific withdrawal symptoms).

- *Dependence* and *abuse* refer to physiological and behavioral symptoms caused by the substance use that lead to significant impairment or personal distress. Specific symptoms of dependence and abuse can be found in the sections that follow.

Symptoms of Substance Dependence

DSM-IV-TR has seven criteria for substance dependence that define a maladaptive pattern of substance use leading to significant impairment or personal distress. Three of the seven criteria must be met within a 12-month period for substance dependence to be diagnosed:

- Criterion 1—tolerance. This is the need for markedly increased amounts of the substance to achieve intoxication or the desired effect, or a markedly diminished effect with continued use of the same amount of a substance.

- Criterion 2—withdrawal. This is characterized by a specific withdrawal syndrome for a particular substance when the client stops completely or reduces the amount used, or the use of the same or a similar substance to relieve or avoid withdrawal symptoms.

- Criterion 3—loss of control. This involves taking the substance in larger amounts or over a longer period than was intended.

- Criterion 4—inability to cut down or control substance use. This involves a persistent desire or unsuccessful efforts to cut down or control substance use.

- Criterion 5—preoccupation or compulsion. This involves spending a great deal of time obtaining the substance, using the substance, or recovering from its effects.

- Criterion 6—psychosocial impairment. This involves reducing or giving up important social, occupational, or recreational activities because of substance use.

- Criterion 7—continued use despite adverse effects. This refers to continuation of substance use despite knowing that a persistent or recurrent physical or psychological problem is probably caused or exacerbated by the substance use.

The *DMS-IV-TR* criteria can be met with or without physiological dependence. If a client meets the first or second diagnostic criterion (tolerance or withdrawal), the diagnosis is specified "with physiological dependence." Other diagnostic specifications include early full remission, early partial remission, sustained full remission, sustained partial remission, on agonist therapy (e.g., methadone maintenance), and in a controlled environment (e.g., prison, therapeutic community, hospital).

A client with a pattern of substance use that does not meet the criteria for dependence but leads to significant impairment or distress is diagnosed with substance abuse if one or more of the following four *DSM-IV-TR* criteria are met within a 12-month period:

- Criterion 1—failure to fulfill major role obligations. This includes obligations at work, home, or school. Examples include repeated absences or poor performance at school or work, suspensions or expulsions from school, or neglect of children or household responsibilities.

- Criterion 2—use in situations in which it is physically hazardous. This includes driving a vehicle or operating a machine when impaired by substance use.

- Criterion 3—legal problems. This includes recurrent, substance-related legal problems such as arrests for disorderly conduct and driving under the influence of alcohol or drugs.

- Criterion 4—continued use despite problems. This involves the continued use of substances despite persistent or recurrent social or interpersonal problems, such as marital conflict or physical fights that are caused or exacerbated by the substance use.

Harmful Consequences

Substance use can contribute directly and indirectly to a multiplicity of problems in any area of functioning. Substance abuse and dependence raise the risk of medical, psychological, psychiatric, family, and economic problems. As shown in Figure 2.1, substance use problems can be classified along a continuum from mild to life-threatening. Accidents, injuries, diseases, suicides, and homicides make substance abuse or dependence fatal for many. The severity of problems varies among individuals in the different areas of functioning. Sometimes the adverse effects of substance use are subtle or hidden. For example, an attorney with alcohol dependence initially reported that her work was not affected by her drinking.

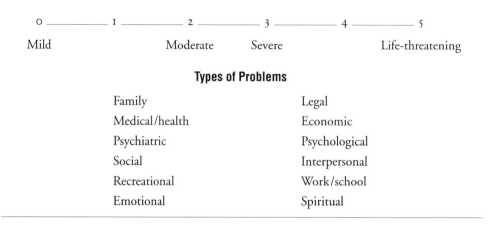

Severity of Problem

0 ——— 1 ——— 2 ——— 3 ——— 4 ——— 5

Mild   Moderate   Severe   Life-threatening

Types of Problems

Family   Legal
Medical/health   Economic
Psychiatric   Psychological
Social   Interpersonal
Recreational   Work/school
Emotional   Spiritual

Figure 2.1

Continuum of substance use problems

However, upon close examination with her therapist, she discovered that her billable hours had actually decreased by about 15% as her drinking worsened.

Table 2.1 summarizes some of the more common problems reported in the clinical and research literature as well as problems that clients have reported to us during assessment or treatment sessions. The number and severity of problems associated with substance use disorders will vary among clients. Also, it is not unusual for a client, even one who is mandated to attend treatment by the court system or by an employer, to minimize adverse affects of substance use. Therefore, the clinician should not expect the client to be forthcoming with substance use problems in the initial sessions. Although psychological defenses may account for denial or minimization, some clients have never examined their problems closely enough to know that these were caused or worsened by substance use.

Perceived Positive Effects of Substances

Despite the problems caused by substance use, clients perceive positive benefits. Such positive expectancies are closely linked to psychological dependence on substances. These include euphorigenic and relaxation

Table 2.1 Problems Associated with Substance Use Disorders

Type of Problem	Example
Medical/health	Accidents; injuries; poor nutrition; weight gain or loss; poor dental hygiene; increased risk of liver, heart, kidney, or lung diseases; cancers of the mouth or pharynx; gastritis; edema; high blood pressure; sexual dysfunction; complications with menstrual cycle, pregnancy, or childbirth; increased risk of AIDS; premature death
Emotional	Anxiety; panic reactions; depression; mood swings; psychosis; suicidal thoughts, feelings, or behaviors; unpredictable behaviors; aggressiveness; violence; self-harm; feelings of shame and guilt; low self-esteem
Work/school	Poor performance; lost jobs or dropping out of school; missing work or school; being undependable and less effective; loss of interest; ruined career; lost opportunities
Family	Lost relationships due to separation, divorce, or involvement of child welfare agencies; family distress and conflict; damaged family relationships; emotional burden on the family (anger, hurt, distrust, fear, worry, depression); poor communication
Interpersonal	Lost or damaged friendships; interpersonal conflicts and dissatisfaction; loss of trust or respect of significant others
Recreational	Diminished interest in or loss of important hobbies, avocations, or other leisure activities
Legal	Fines; legal constraints; arrests; convictions; jail or prison time; probation or parole
Economic	Loss of income; excessive debts; loan defaults or ignoring other financial obligations; loss of security or living arrangements; inability to take care of basic needs for food or shelter; using up all financial resources; inability to manage money

effects, in which clients enjoy the euphoria or the "high" of the substance as well as the feeling of being "chilled out" or relaxed after using. Some clients also report feeling more energetic, interpersonally attractive, sexual, perceptive, or creative as a result of their substance use. Others perceive the benefits of substance use in terms of helping them blot out or escape from their problems or numb their uncomfortable feelings. Even when there are many adverse effects, clients will be able to articulate perceived positive effects of using substances, which reinforces continued use. Understanding substance use from the client's perspective helps the therapist or counselor to be sensitive to the client's perceived positive benefits of using. The Decision-Making Matrix in Chapter 7 (see Figure

7.1 in Chapter 7 of this guide and Chapter 5 in the Workbook) provides one clinical tool for helping clients identify both positive and negative aspects of substance use.

Effects of Substance Use Problems on the Family

Alcohol and drug problems often have a negative effect on the family (CSAT, 2004b; Daley & Miller, 2001; NIDA, 2003; Nunes et al., 2000; Parran, Leipman, & Farkas, 2003; Stanton & Heath, 2005; Tarter et al., 1995). Family relationships are lost due to separation, divorce, or the involvement of child welfare agencies. Families feel neglected, and in some cases their basic needs for food, shelter, and clothing are ignored. The economic burden can be tremendous as a result of family income going for the purchase of drugs or alcohol; lost income due to impairment caused by substance use; and costs associated with legal, medical, or psychiatric problems. Family members often feel an emotional burden as well. Anger, fear, worry, distrust, and depression are common. Episodes of neglect, abuse, or violence are often associated with alcohol and other drug abuse. Substance use disorders make it difficult if not impossible to function responsibly as a parent or spouse, which leads to problems in specific family relationships. Due to the genetic predisposition associated with substance use disorders and faulty role modeling, children of parents who have alcohol or drug problems are more vulnerable than other children to developing their own substance use problems (Moss et al., 1995; Tarter et al., 1995).

Case Examples

The following cases provide specific examples of alcohol abuse, tobacco and alcohol dependence, and opiate dependence with polydrug abuse. These brief cases illustrate how substance use disorders vary in terms of symptoms, severity, and adverse effects on the client and family.

Randy (Alcohol Abuse)

■ *Randy is a 41-year-old, married father of two with a 16-year history of alcohol use. He owns a small home-improvement business and employs four other men. Randy first drank at age 15 and first became intoxicated at age 17. He drank moderately until his early 30s, at which time he increased the frequency and amount of alcohol intake from several drinks per month to regular weekend use of six or more beers, and occasional weekday use of four or more beers per drinking occasion. During the past year and a half, Randy has had several weekend binges leading to bad hangovers, causing him to miss work and pay less attention to his business than usual. He and his wife began arguing over his alcohol use and his failure to spend time with her and the children on weekends. Often on weekends, after going to potential customers' homes to give estimates, Randy stops at local bars and clubs and drinks with his friends.* ■

Nicole (Tobacco and Alcohol Dependence)

■ *Nicole is a 55-year-old, divorced mother of two adult children and grandmother of five. She had over 30 years of alcohol dependence. Nicole drank on a daily basis, consuming up to a case of beer at a time during her worst period of drinking. Her tolerance was quite high for many years, although in the final years of drinking her tolerance actually decreased. She also experienced withdrawal tremors and would often drink in the morning to stop them. Her alcohol use contributed to severe family conflict, an inability to function as an effective mother when her children were young, financial problems, depression, suicidal feelings, and an inability to hold a job. Nicole has been sober for over 1 year and her life has improved modestly. She now wants to address her dependence on nicotine. She has been smoking two to three packs of cigarettes a day for "too many years to count." Nicole reports that her dependence on nicotine has caused her to have problems with shortness of breath when walks long distances or up stairs, has made her more susceptible to a variety of minor physical ailments, has been a factor in heated arguments with one of her adult sons (who refuses to bring his children to visit her "smoke-filled house"), and is using up too much of her limited income.* ■

Steve (Opiate Dependence and Polydrug Abuse)

Steve is a 36-year-old, divorced physician who began using alcohol and marijuana during high school. His use increased during college and medical school, but he managed to make excellent grades, mainly due to his intellectual ability. During the latter part of his medical internship, Steve began snorting heroin and cocaine occasionally. This pattern continued fairly steadily when he joined a medical practice. During the past several years, Steve used Percocet on a daily basis. He also began shooting heroin intravenously and couldn't function without opiates in his system. Steve used a variety of other drugs to reduce his anxiety and insomnia and stress. However, drugs eventually became the central organizing factor in his life. Prior to entering treatment involuntarily, his drug dependence cost him his marriage. To continue practicing medicine, he is required by a state regulatory agency to maintain abstinence from all illicit drugs and alcohol, participate in treatment, and submit regular urine samples to verify his abstinence.

Chapter 3 | *Assessment of Substance Use Problems*

Areas of Assessment

The assessment of substance use disorders differs from other mental health assessments in that detailed information is obtained on patterns of alcohol or other drug use, effects of use, potential effects of substances on other psychiatric disorders, current withdrawal potential, and attitudes and beliefs about continued use and abstinence.

Pattern of Substance Use

The therapist should determine the client's current (past several months) and historical pattern of substance use (amount and frequency of use in each category of substances), methods of use (e.g., intravenous, intramuscular, intranasal, oral), periods of non-use or non-problematic use, and perceived reasons for using alcohol or other drugs. The therapist asks how the client acquires substances, how much money is spent on them, the interpersonal and social context of substance use, and whether the client mixes substances to "boost" the effects. If the client injects drugs, the therapist can ask if he or she shares needles, cotton, or rinsing water with other drug users, as sharing any of these items increases the chances of acquiring or transmitting the AIDS virus.

Symptoms of Substance Use Disorders

The therapist determines how the substance use pattern presented relates to the *DSM-IV-TR* symptoms of various disorders (abuse, dependence, withdrawal, etc.). Is there evidence of tolerance or physical withdrawal, obsessions or compulsions to use, or psychosocial impairment?

Effects of Substance Use

The therapist asks the client about problems caused or worsened by substance use or related behaviors. These problems may be in any area of functioning: medical or physical, psychological or emotional, work or school, family, interpersonal, recreational, legal, spiritual, or economic. In the initial assessment period, clients are often not aware of or minimize the adverse effects of substance use on themselves and others. The therapist may identify more specific effects in subsequent assessment and treatment sessions by having the client complete the Harmful Effects Worksheet (see Figure 3.1 in this guide and Chapter 3 in the workbook), which asks the client to list problems caused by substance use as they relate to every major domain of functioning.

Psychological or Psychiatric Problems

The therapist asks if the client is currently experiencing serious psychiatric or psychological problems such as depression; mania; anxiety; phobias; obsessions or compulsions; psychosis; suicidal thoughts; homicidal thoughts; self-destructive behaviors (e.g., cutting or burning self); violent aggressive behaviors; problems with compulsive eating, gambling, or sex; or problems with bingeing and purging. The therapist asks if the client is experiencing any upsetting feelings resulting from prior traumatic experiences, such as being a victim of incest, sexual abuse, or violence or witnessing unusual events such as combat or horrible disasters. If symptoms or problems are currently endorsed, the therapist can ask how long they have been present and how much they bother the client in order to determine subjective distress. The therapist asks the client how his or her substance use affects the symptoms and how he or she thinks the symptoms affect substance use. Is there any family history of psychiatric illness or any prior treatment received by the client for a non-substance use problem (e.g., inpatient psychiatric hospital, partial hospital program, community residential program, outpatient therapy, pharmacotherapy)? What did the client find helpful or unhelpful about prior treatment experiences? Chapters 16 and 17 review assessment and treatment strategies for co-occurring psychiatric disorders in greater detail.

Harmful Effects Worksheet

Problems Caused by or Worsened by Your Substance Use

Instructions: In the sections below, list any problems that you think were caused by or worsened by your alcohol, tobacco, or drug problem in the past year. Then, rank each of the eight categories from the most severe to the least severe, using "1" for the most severe category of problems.

Medical/physical/dental
_____5_____

Lost weight

Poor dental hygiene

Hurt in auto accident and a fall

Psychological or emotional
_____1_____

Felt like a nobody

Depressed

Work/school
_____4_____

Work at 80% capacity

Used all my sick days up

Quit night school, didn't get my degree

Family
_____2_____

Wife and kids are upset and disappointed in me

Parents are heartbroken

Interpersonal relationships
_____7_____

Friend, John, upset with me

Recreational
_____8_____

Bored with events where I couldn't drink

Gave up playing sports

Legal
_____3_____

Charged with driving under the influence of alcohol

Economic
_____6_____

Spent too much money to count on booze

Created financial problems for family

Never saved for the future

Figure 3.1

Example of a completed Harmful Effects Worksheet.

Medical and Sexual History

The therapist inquires about current or past medical or dental problems, medications currently used, allergies, or adverse reactions to medications. Is there any significant family medical history? What is the client's sexual preference? Is there any history of sexual problems or high-risk behaviors, such as intravenous drug use, unprotected sex, or sex with multiple partners, that increase the client's chance of being HIV positive?

Psychosocial History

The therapist asks about the client's relationships with family (parents and siblings, spouse, children) and friends. The therapist also asks about the client's academic, work, financial, and legal histories; hobbies and avocations; and religious preferences.

Motivation to Change

The therapist inquires why the client is seeking help and what the client wants to change about his or her substance use. Motivation may be external (e.g., legal system, employer, family, significant other), internal, or a combination of both. Clients often initially seek help as a result of some external pressure. As part of the initial assessment, the client can complete the Self-Rating Scale (see Figure 3.2 in this guide and Chapter 2 in the Workbook). On the Self-Rating Scale, the client rates the severity of the substance use problem and the level of his or her motivation to quit substance use. The therapist should determine which stage of change the client is in: precontemplation, contemplation, preparation, action, maintenance, or termination (DiClemente, 2003; Prochaska, 2003; Prochaska & DiClemente, 1992).

Past History of Treatment and Use of Self-Help Programs

The therapist gathers information about the client's prior involvement in substance abuse treatment (e.g., detoxification; inpatient or outpatient rehabilitation program; partial hospital or intensive outpatient program;

Self-Rating Scale

Instructions: After reviewing your pattern of substance use and the consequences, rate the current severity of your problem. Then rate your current level of motivation to quit using substances and confidence level to maintain your sobriety.

Severity Level of My Problem

My Motivation Level to Quit Using Substances

My Confidence in My Ability to Stay Sober

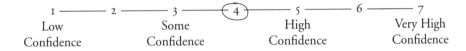

Figure 3.2
Example of a completed Self-Rating Scale.

therapeutic community; halfway house; outpatient or aftercare counseling; self-help groups such as Alcoholics Anonymous, Narcotics Anonymous, Cocaine Anonymous, Rational Recovery, Self-Management and Recovery Training (SMART), Women for Sobriety, Moderation Management, or any other self-help program). What is the client's perception of the effectiveness of prior treatments, and what did the client find helpful or unhelpful? The therapist also inquires about the client's past use of pharmacotherapeutic agents for detoxification or ongoing treatment (e.g., methadone, naltrexone, bromocriptine, amantadine, disulfiram).

History of Attempts to Quit Without Help

The therapist asks the client about past attempts at quitting substance use without help. Many clients have quit cigarette, alcohol, or drug use on their own without the help of professionals, medications, or self-help groups. If the client did quit without help, what cognitive, behavioral, or other strategies did he or she use?

Coping Skills

The therapist assesses the client's style of coping with problems, stress, and upsetting feelings. Does the client blame others for his or her difficulties or accept responsibility? Does the client cope with distress by using alcohol or other drugs? What kinds of cognitive strategies does the client typically use (e.g., self-reflection, challenging and changing beliefs or thinking, positive self-talk)? What behavioral strategies does the client usually use (e.g., avoidance, testing out new behaviors, monitoring specific behaviors or actions)? What interpersonal tactics does the client use (e.g., reaching out for social support, sharing problems and feelings with a confidant, talking through problems at self-help meetings)? What spiritual strategies does the client use (e.g., prayer, mediation, participation in formal religious activities)?

Social Support System

The therapist assesses whether the client has supportive family or friends. Does he or she have one or more confidants? Are current relationships satisfying? Is the client able to give and receive support from significant others and manage interpersonal conflict? Is the client involved with a partner or friends who actively abuse alcohol or other drugs? Does the client have significant others who are likely to exert pressure to use alcohol or drugs?

Strengths and Resiliencies

Assess the client's view of his personal strengths and resiliencies. How does he or she describe his or her positive qualities and strengths or abilities related to work, relationships, learning, avocations, or other areas of life? Is the client resilient and able to bounce back from adversity or setbacks?

Methods of Assessment

To complete the assessment, the therapist can use clinical or collateral interviews, pen-and-paper tests, urinalysis or breathalyzer screenings, laboratory tests, or prior treatment records. Specific methods used depend on the therapist's preferences, the reason the client is seeking help, and the system in which the therapist works. Supplemental sources of information such as laboratory tests and collateral interviews are especially helpful when the client is perceived not to be providing accurate information.

Clinical Interviews

Clinical interviews can be conducted to determine if the client meets any of the symptoms of a substance use disorder according to *DSM-IV-TR*. Interviews can also be conducted by using structured instruments such as the Addiction Severity Index (ASI; McLellan, 1985). There are 7-day and 30-day versions of the ASI that can be used to assess the client at various points in the treatment process. Clinical interviews can also be semi-structured, covering a broad range of areas such as those discussed in the previous section.

Collateral Interviews

It is sometimes helpful and necessary to gather additional information from people who are familiar with the client and his or her problems. Family members, significant others, or professionals (e.g., probation officer, family physician) may provide important information about the client. Collateral interviews are often helpful when the client is seeking help for an external reason. Due to stringent federal and state confidentiality guidelines related to releasing information on clients with alcohol or other drug problems, the therapist must first get the client's written permission to obtain information from or share information with family, significant others, prior counselors or therapists, or others involved with the client (e.g., criminal justice, social service, or healthcare professionals).

Pen-and-Paper Tests

Brief questionnaires such as the *Michigan Alcoholism Screening Test* (Selzer, 1971), *Drug Abuse Screening Test* (Skinner, 1982), or the *Simple Screening Instrument for Substance Abuse* (CSAT, 1994) can be used to supplement data gained from clinical interviews. More comprehensive questionnaires, such as the Alcohol Use Disorders Identification Test (AUDIT) (Allen et al., 1977) and the *Drug Use Screening Inventory* (Tarter, 1990), can be used to gather more detailed information to use in prioritizing problems and determining the treatment needs of a client. There are also questionnaires that help measure treatment readiness, risk for AIDS, cravings for substances, and involvement in self-help programs. Although these and other questionnaires are often used in treatment-research clinical trials, they can be helpful to the therapist as well. It is most appropriate to administer these questionnaires during the assessment process, as they can be used by the treating therapist to provide feedback to the client. Substance-related questionnaires can be used when clients enter treatment, as well as at various points in time during treatment (e.g., 30 or 90 days). (For more information on screening instruments, see APA, 2000b; CSAT, 1994; NIAAA, 2005).

Withdrawal Scales

Clinician-administered scales are available to assess alcohol withdrawal (*Clinical Institute Withdrawal Assessment;* CIWA-Ar) or opiate withdrawal (*Opiate Withdrawal Assessment;* OWA). Scores from the CIWA-AR or OWA help physicians and nurses know when to administer medications to attenuate substance withdrawal symptoms (APA, 2000b).

Urinalysis and Breathalyzer Screenings

Urinalysis and breathalyzer screenings can be used during the initial assessment, regularly or as needed throughout the course of treatment, or randomly. This type of screening helps determine recent use of substances, helps monitor the client's progress in treatment or difficulty staying sober, and provides an external control for abstinence that many clients find helpful. Regular urinalysis and breathalyzer screenings can be especially helpful in eliminating controversy over whether a specific client who was mandated for treatment has used substances. For example, healthcare professionals, athletes, attorneys, bus drivers, court-mandated clients, and others who are mandated for treatment are frequently required to submit urine samples as a way of monitoring sobriety. These screenings can actually protect such individuals in the event they are falsely accused of using substances. There are various types of tests available, including thin-layer chromatography (TLC), enzyme immunoassay (EIA), enzyme multiplied immunoassay test (EMIT), radioimmunoassay (RIA), fluorescent polarization immunoassay (FPIA), and gas-liquid chromatography (GLC).

Laboratory Tests

Laboratory tests can be used to help screen for alcohol problems because serum assays can be elevated by excessive drinking. However, problem drinkers can have normal scores, so a normal score cannot be interpreted as an absence of physical damage from drinking. Tests such as plasma gamma-glutamyl transferase (GGT) and mean corpuscular volume measure injury to the liver and the cells that manufacture red blood cells. Other tests, such as the plasma carbohydrate-deficient transferrin (CDT) test, measure nonspecific alcohol-related changes rather than organ damage. An HIV test, a hepatitis antigen and antibody test, or other tests (e.g., pregnancy test, tuberculin skin test, chest X-ray) may be used based on the circumstances of the client.

Prior Treatment Records

Records of previous treatment experiences or records from another significant source (e.g., probation officer, EAP evaluator) can provide additional information about the client.

Treatment goals need to be negotiated with each client. They are based on current problems, motivation to change, and perceived needs for treatment. In many instances the assessment will provide sufficient information to document a substance dependence or abuse problem. In these cases abstinence should be encouraged by the clinician even if the client does not agree with this goal. In such cases, the clinician can provide specific feedback as to why abstinence is recommended. However, there will be instances in which a client does not meet the criteria for substance abuse or dependency yet is having some problems with substance use. Although many clients will identify abstinence from substances as their desired goal, others may prefer only to reduce their harmful use of substances. Some nondependent clients may successfully learn to moderate their use, but others will learn that they cannot do this for an extended period of time.

Many clients are ambivalent about their choice of treatment goals and the motivation required to attain these goals. For some, the options are dichotomous: either one pursues an abstinence-only goal or one continues to drink or use drugs at one's current level despite the problems involved. This is similar to seeing the goals as similar to a traffic light that is either red (stop drinking) or green (keep drinking and don't stop). Those who are unwilling or unable to stop often give up or drop out of any treatment that does not allow for any use. For these clients, the option of a harm-reduction goal is similar to the yellow light, which signals the driver to slow down, proceed with caution, and be aware of the risks involved prior to moving forward at a reduced pace. After experiencing success with such a "slow-down" approach, clients often gain confidence in their ability to make changes in their high-risk behavior without giving up or dropping out. Often this "step-down" approach will motivate the client to try giving up all use as an eventual (although perhaps delayed) treatment goal. Clients who are unable to moderate their use successfully may be more likely to embrace the goal of abstinence as a result.

Case Examples

The following cases provide examples of four different individuals who sought treatment for problems with alcohol or other drugs. These cases clearly illustrate that the actual effects of substance use problems may vary significantly among individuals.

Tracy (Mild Effects)

Tracy is a 28-year-old, married, employed mother of two children who has a 6-year history of alcohol and marijuana abuse. Tracy is in good physical health and has had no major problems from her substance use. However, she reports that her occasional bouts of intoxication lead to arguments with her husband, and that she feels guilty for embarrassing herself and her family. Tracy was also involved in a minor car accident while under the influence of marijuana.

Don (Moderate Effects)

Don is a 49-year-old college professor and married father of two adult children. He has had an alcohol problem for the past 10 years and has twice successfully completed rehabilitation programs, leading to periods of abstinence of several years or longer. His most recent relapse came after 30 months of continuous sobriety. Although he is tenured at the college where he teaches, he feels pressure to maintain his sobriety because his last binge affected his ability to teach, and the dean of his department pressured him to seek professional help again. Don reports that his wife is worried about and upset with him, and his children are disappointed that he relapsed. He feels guilty and ashamed that he had to return to treatment after doing so well for several years. Don's latest relapse was also a factor in an episode of depression.

George (Severe Effects)

George is a 41-year old, unemployed, divorced father of three children with a 23-history of alcoholism, heroin dependence, tobacco dependence, and crack cocaine abuse. George's wife left him over 15 years ago after he was arrested and spent time in jail for burglary. He became involved in crime at that time to support an expensive daily heroin addiction. Although George has not used any opiate drug in the past 11 years, his drinking has increased considerably. More recently, he also started using crack cocaine. George states that his addiction has led to many serious problems in his life. These include losing several relationships with women; being a victim of a robbery and violent beatings on at least three occasions; getting kicked out of apartments many times, leading to periods of homelessness; poor nutrition, leading to loss of weight, dental problems, and poor physical health; gastritis caused by excessive drinking; gout; chronic obstructive pulmonary disease caused by excessive smoking; losing many jobs and being unable to work; and numerous arrests for public intoxication and for selling drugs. George has been in jail several times, hospitalized for complications of his alcoholism four times, hospitalized in a psychiatric facility twice following suicidal feelings after going on crack cocaine runs, detoxified in hospitals and Salvation Army social detoxification centers more than 20 times, and treated in addiction rehabilitation programs and halfway house programs at least five times. Whereas he once maintained continuous sobriety for over 2 years, the longest he has been able to stay sober in the past 5 years has been 3 months. ▪

Liane (Co-occurring Disorders)

▪ *Liane is a 43-year-old housewife with two children, both boys entering their teen-age years. Although she has a doctoral degree in biology, she agreed to be a "stay-at-home mom" while her husband worked as a college professor. She had a chronic problem with both depression and alcohol dependence and was told by her psychiatrist that she needed to pursue abstinence from all alcohol use before he would continue her psychotherapy for depression. She then completed an intake in an alcoholism center with abstinence as the only treatment option. She was told by the intake worker that her depression was caused by her alcohol dependence, even though her psychiatrist had suggested it was the other way around (she was drinking to self-medicate her depression). Liane reported that both accounts held merit, in that she often drank to cope with her feelings of depression, but would then feel even more guilty and depressed as a result of falling into this vicious cycle often associated with a dual disorder problem. She felt "caught in the middle" between the mental health and addiction treatment fields and was eager to embrace an integrated treatment approach that would deal with both problems. From her motivational perspective, she was not yet ready to give up drinking since it was the only source of relief that she could count on, at least in the short run. (Her position reflects a basic assumption of the harm-reduction approach: do not take a client's main coping strategy away until alternative skills are in place.)*

Liane agreed to enter an integrated outpatient treatment program that would address both her drinking and depression problems. After keeping track of both her alcohol consumption and related mood states, she could get a "bigger picture" of the functional relationship between them. After several months of therapy, she also acquired an interest in meditation and attended a mindfulness training retreat for a 2-week period. During the retreat, she took the precept not to use any intoxicants that would cloud her thinking and obscure her awareness. After the retreat, she reported success in using meditation to cope with her depression and associated alcohol cravings. As she put it, "since the meditation program, I now realize that I no longer am dictated to by my thoughts, including urges and cravings to drink. I just accept these longings, let go of them, and move on." Liane has not had any alcohol since treatment ended more than 4 years ago. She was able to change her goal from harm reduction to abstinence thanks to the support of her therapist, who was willing to support her even though her treatment goals changed over time. ▪

Treatment Settings and Approaches

Chapter 4 | *Treatment Settings for Substance Use Problems*

(Corresponds to chapter 4 of the workbook)

Introduction

Effective work with clients who have substance use problems requires the therapist to be aware of and able to use a broad range of treatment resources. In this chapter, a range of treatment settings is briefly discussed.

In general, the least restrictive level of treatment should be used unless the severity of the substance use disorder and related medical, psychiatric, and social problems is such that structured or medically monitored treatment is needed. Therapists are encouraged to become familiar with the American Society on Addiction Medicine (ASAM, 2001, 2003) criteria so they can make appropriate decisions on what level of care to seek for a given client. ASAM delineates five levels of care:

- Level 0.5—early intervention

- Level 1—outpatient services

- Level 2—intensive outpatient (IOP) or partial hospitalization (PH) services

- Level 3—residential or inpatient services

- Level 4—medically managed intensive inpatient treatment

ASAM uses specific criteria along six different dimensions to determine the most appropriate level of care. These dimensions are acute intoxication and/or withdrawal potential, biomedical conditions and complications, emotional or behavioral conditions and complications, treatment acceptance or resistance, relapse potential, and recovery environment.

Early Intervention (Level 0.5)

This level of intervention refers to "pre-treatment" approaches, which may or may not lead to the individual engaging in professional care. An example is a driving under the influence program or other service for individuals at risk for developing a substance problem, or for whom there is not enough information to document a disorder at the current time.

Outpatient and Aftercare Programs (Level 1)

These programs vary in length from several weeks to months or longer. They may precede or follow rehabilitation programs or be used as the sole treatment. Their purpose is to help the client achieve and maintain abstinence or reduce harmful substance use, as well as make personal changes to facilitate ongoing recovery and minimize relapse risk. Individual, group, and family therapy; pharmacotherapy; and other ancillary services may be offered, depending on the specific setting. Outpatient treatment is most suitable for clients who are not at risk for withdrawal complications, have a stable medical and mental condition, show a willingness to cooperate with treatment, are able to maintain abstinence with minimal support, and have a supportive recovery environment.

Non-Residential Addiction Rehabilitation Programs (Level 2)

These short-term (2 to 6 weeks) programs include intensive outpatient and partial hospital programs. These programs provide addiction and recovery education and treatment to clients who do not need the supervision and structure of a residential or hospital-based program. These are sometimes used as "step-down" programs for clients who have received treatment in a residential addiction program or hospital-based program, or as "step-up" programs for clients who started treatment in a more traditional outpatient program but were unable to make sufficient progress. These programs are appropriate for clients who have minimal withdrawal risk, have no serious medical conditions, have high enough resistance to recovery to require a structured treatment program, are likely to relapse without close monitoring and support, and have an unsupportive environment.

Although managed care has led to a significant decrease in the availability of inpatient and residential programs for substance use disorders, a wide range of options is still available. Options include both hospital-based and non–hospital-based residential programs. Some are "generic" in the sense that as long as a client meets the program's criteria, he or she can be admitted to the program. Others are specialized and serve specific populations based on type and severity of addiction, gender, family status, or ethnicity. Following is a brief description of inpatient programs.

Short-Term Addiction Rehabilitation Programs

The traditional 28-day rehabilitation program has changed drastically. Most programs now offer a variable length of stay, with many clients staying less than 14 days. Unless there are serious co-existing medical or psychiatric problems, non–hospital-based programs are the first choice for rehabilitation. Addiction rehabilitation programs are usually recommended if clients have been unable to initiate and sustain recovery through less intensive treatment settings such as outpatient, intensive outpatient, or partial hospital programs. They may also be used if the addiction is of such severity that a period of time in a structured, residential setting is needed to break the cycle of addiction and help motivate the client to establish a foundation for recovery. Short-term rehab programs are also appropriate for clients who have a high relapse potential, who are in environments considered dangerous for recovery, or who do not have access to outpatient rehabilitation.

Long-Term Addiction Rehabilitation Programs

Some clients with severe patterns of addiction and serious psychosocial impairment (e.g., no social support, lack of vocational skills, history of multiple relapses, serious problems with the legal system) need long-term programs (several months to a year or longer) to maintain sobriety and address important lifestyle and personality issues. Long-term rehab programs include therapeutic communities, halfway houses, and specialized programs dealing with specific populations such as men, women, women with children, specific ethnic groups, clients involved with the criminal justice system as a result of substance-related problems, and others. The trend is toward shorter-term programs. For example, therapeutic community programs that once were up to 2 years in length are now several months to less than a year in duration.

Detoxification (Levels 3 and 4)

Detoxification refers to the process of tapering the client off alcohol or other drugs. Medical detoxification may be provided in an addiction rehabilitation facility, psychiatric hospital, or medical hospital. Medical detoxification is indicated if there is a documented history or current evidence of withdrawal complications such as seizures, delirium tremens (DTs), or serious suicidal feelings. In contemporary practice, medical detoxification normally takes up to several days. Detoxification from severe dependence on opiates or benzodiazepines may be initiated in a detoxification program, continued in outpatient or partial hospital treatment, and last several weeks or longer.

Some clients benefit from "social detoxification" programs in which supportive care, rest, and nutrition are offered. Referrals are made to medical facilities in cases of complicated withdrawal. Social detoxification programs are usually provided for chronic substance users from lower socioeconomic groups.

Outpatient detoxification is appropriate for clients with less severe forms of substance use disorders who do not show any evidence of serious substance-related medical or psychiatric problems and who have support from family or other significant people. Counseling is usually provided with medical management.

Detoxification involves providing medications to attenuate withdrawal symptoms. Detoxification is of limited value if it is not followed by other forms of treatment such as rehabilitation or outpatient care. Although there is not a standard approach to detoxification, specific protocols do exist that outline when to use, increase, or decrease medication. Chapter 6 provides information on medications used in detoxification from different substances.

Special Programs

Other specialized treatment programs include those designed specifically for smoking cessation, those designed as part of a treatment-research protocol to study a specific type of outpatient psychosocial treatment (e.g., coping skills training, relapse prevention) or pharmacotherapy, or those designed for clients with dual disorders (e.g., substance use and psychiatric disorders).

Opiate Maintenance Therapy (OMT)

OMTs include methadone maintenance (MM) and buprenorphine maintenance, which are used to help opiate addicts who have been unsuccessful in their attempts to quit (CSAT, 2005a; Pani et al., 2000; Payte, Zweben, & Martin, 2003; Saxon, 2003; Stein, Greenwald, & Kosten, 2003; Thomas, 2001). Provided in conjunction with education and counseling services, OMTs are designed to eventually help wean the client from opiates. However, many clients actually remain on MM for many months, even years. MM helps reduce use of illicit opiates and related criminal behavior and helps opiate addicts function at work and in the community. Despite criticisms, MM is a helpful treatment for addicts who are unable to sustain abstinence from heroin or other opiate drugs.

Buprenorphine (Buprenex, Suboxone, and Subutex) was recently approved by the U.S. Food and Drug Administration in the treatment of opiate addiction. Buprenorphine can be prescribed only by a physician with special certification. It is used in office-based practices and at opiate treatment clinics to help addicted individuals withdraw from opiates, or for maintenance treatment. Buprenorphine is also used in pain management.

Homework for Client

■ Complete the Initial Goals for Treatment Worksheet.

Chapter 5 | *Psychosocial Therapies for Substance Use Disorders*

Introduction

There are a variety of psychosocial therapies and counseling approaches for alcohol, tobacco, and other drug problems. Although some specific treatments have been shown in clinical trials to be more effective than others, to date there is no single, superior treatment approach appropriate for all clients. For example, in a large-scale, multisite study of clients with alcohol problems who were randomly assigned to one of three treatment approaches (cognitive-behavioral coping skills training, motivational enhancement therapy, and 12-step facilitation therapy), it was found that all treatments worked similarly (Project MATCH, 1998). Although clients benefited from all three of these psychosocial treatments, none was significantly superior to the others. All three treatments were provided by trained counselors using a manual-based treatment approach.

Although brief treatments have been successful with less severe types of alcohol problems, longer-term treatments are often needed for drug problems (Onken, Blaine, & Boren, 1997). For many clients, substance use is a chronic disorder requiring long-term involvement in professional treatment, self-help programs, or both (McLellan et al., 2000).

In recent years, a number of specific individual and group treatment approaches have been described in treatment manuals (see CSAT, NIAAA, and NIDA references for these specific treatment approaches). Most of these manuals were initially developed for use in clinical trials and describe the theoretical orientation of the treatment approach, clinical techniques, and recovery issues to address in individual, group, or family sessions.

Table 5.1 Psychosocial Therapies and Approaches

Cognitive and behavioral therapies

Coping and social skill training

Community reinforcement approach

Dual disorder (substance use and psychiatric disorders) therapies

Family and marital therapies

Harm reduction

Individual drug counseling

Group drug counseling

Motivational enhancement therapy

Motivational interviewing

Neurobehavioral model of recovery

Relapse prevention

Social network therapy

12-step facilitation therapy

Table 5.1 shows that there are many different approaches currently used to treat substance use problems. Although a discussion of these various treatment approaches is beyond the scope of this book, the interested reader is encouraged to consult one of the major textbooks on addiction or specific NIAAA or NIDA treatment manuals (these and other resources are listed in References and Suggested Readings).

Client Choice of Treatment Options

Given that the results of Project MATCH did not support the hypothesis that client characteristics would predict who would respond to each of the three treatment approaches for alcohol problems, and given that all approaches did equally well in terms of follow-up results, an alternative approach is recommended: client choice. Since there is no firm evidence that any one particular treatment intervention is more effective than any other, clients could be given a menu of treatment options to choose from (see Table 5.1). To do this effectively, clients need to be educated about the basic principles and assumptions of different treatment models, perhaps by showing them video clips or written protocols that illustrate the range of treatment alternatives. They can be encouraged to select choices that best fit with their own attitudes and personal preferences—as informed consumers. If the client's first-choice program does not work out, the second choice could then be attempted, and so on down the line until a final effective choice is found.

Treatment Principles and Guidelines

Following is a brief summary of treatment principles and guidelines that can serve as a framework for dealing with substance use disorders. These are based on a review of the literature, NIDA's principles (1999b), and our experience in providing clinical care.

1. *Assessment: Initial and Ongoing.* A thorough initial assessment is needed to determine substance use disorder diagnoses, effects of these disorders, specific problems of the client, and treatment goals (Donovan & Marlatt, 2005). Clients should be assessed for HIV/AIDS, hepatitis B and C, tuberculosis, and other infectious diseases (NIDA, 1999b). Clients testing positive can be referred for appropriate medical help and offered psychological counseling to deal with their reaction to having a disease. During ongoing treatment, clients should be monitored continuously for alcohol or drug use and assessed for problems that may require other interventions (e.g., social, family, vocational, housing, financial, spiritual, legal). A variety of assessment strategies can be used to complete a detailed evaluation of each client seeking treatment (see Chapter 3).

2. *Treatment Settings.* There are a variety of treatment settings available for substance use problems. While some clients participate in a single type of treatment setting, others move back and forth among many settings. In general, the least restrictive level of care should be used when feasible. Inpatient or residential programs, for example, should not be routinely used before other levels of treatment have been tried unless the severity of the substance use disorder and concomitant medical or psychiatric problems warrants these levels of care (see Chapter 4). Ideally, treatment needs

to be readily available, but this is not always the case. There are times in which the therapist or a case manager (if available) will have to negotiate other systems on behalf of the client.

3. *Therapeutic Alliance.* Establishing and maintaining a therapeutic alliance is essential in helping the client engage in treatment, remain in treatment long enough to benefit from it, and adhere to the individualized treatment plan (Onken, Blaine, & Boren, 1997; Petry & Bickel, 1999). The clinician must be aware of both helpful and unhelpful attitudes and behaviors that affect the therapeutic alliance with substance abusers.

4. *Client Motivation.* Since clients are often reluctant to enter treatment, the clinician needs to have strategies to motivate them to enter and remain in treatment. Many clients enter treatment as a result of external motivation or pressure. Treatment does not have to be voluntary to be effective (NIDA, 2000a). Motivational and compliance-enhancing approaches can be used to help engage and keep clients in treatment (e.g., CSAT, 1999b; Daley & Zuckoff, 1999; Miller & Rollnick, 2002; Swanson et al., 2002; Ziedonis & Trudeau, 1997; Zuckoff & Daley, 2001). Outreach efforts are often needed to re-engage early treatment dropouts.

5. *Flexibility.* A flexible approach to treatment is needed. If one type of program or intervention is minimally effective or ineffective, other approaches should be considered. Psychosocial, pharmacologic, and self-help programs all are valuable approaches for substance use disorders. Changes should be made to a treatment plan based on the client's progress or lack of progress. The focus of treatment should be dynamic and shift based on changes in the client's problems or circumstances. For example, a client sober from alcohol who develops an episode of clinical depression would benefit from treatment addressing the mood disorder. A client unable to establish abstinence from cocaine with weekly outpatient therapy may need referral to a higher level of care, such as a residential, partial hospital, or intensive outpatient program. Or an opiate addict unable to remain drug-free while participating in psychosocial treatments may benefit from pharmacotherapy (e.g., methadone maintenance or buprenorphine).

6. *Time in Treatment.* Treatment is effective to the extent that the client remains long enough to benefit from it, particularly for drug dependence (NIDA, 1999b). For many, drug dependence is a long-term, chronic condition that often requires the client to remain in treatment for a minimum of 90 days, especially for outpatient care. Brief interventions are most effective for alcohol use disorders and problem drinking among college students (Baer et al., 2001; Bien, Miller, & Tonigan, 1993; CSAT, 1999a).

7. *Treatment Modalities.* A single treatment modality is seldom effective. Often clients need a combination of treatments such as therapy along with self-help meetings, or therapy, medications, and self-help meetings. Psychosocial treatments (e.g., therapy or "programs") can be used alone, in combination (e.g., individual and group counseling), or in combination with medications and mutual support groups. Some treatment modalities such as detoxification have limited value if not followed with involvement in other forms of care, such as residential, partial hospital, or intensive outpatient programs.

8. *Medications Help Many Clients, Especially When Combined With Psychosocial Treatments.* Medications (see Chapter 6) can be used to help clients safely withdrawal from addictive substances, help with their ongoing recovery (e.g., ReVia or Campral for alcohol dependence, Trexan for opiate dependence), as replacements to highly addictive substances (e.g., methadone or buprenorphine as a substitute for heroin, or nicotine replacements), or for treatment of co-occurring medical or psychiatric disorders (e.g., antidepressants for depression or mood stabilizers for bipolar illness). Assessing the need for medications and monitoring adherence are important tasks of the therapist.

9. *Treatment Phases.* There are different phases or stages of recovery from a substance use disorder (Connors, Donovan, & DiClemente, 2001; Prochaska & DiClemente, 1992; Rawson et al., 2005). Recovery is not a linear process, so clients do not smoothly go from one phase to the other. And since many clients lapse or relapse, they move back and forth between the various phases. The stages-of-change paradigm provides a broad-based framework that con-

siders time in treatment and specific recovery issues. The goals of treatment will change depending on which stage a client is in and the specific problems and challenges he or she is facing (see Chapter 7).

10. *Treatment Issues.* Recovery is a process that involves change in substance use as well as other areas of functioning. The specific changes that each client attempts to make may occur in any major domain of functioning—physical, emotional, family, social and interpersonal, spiritual, and other (see Chapter 8). For maximum effectiveness, treatment should address other problems and needs of the client, not just the substance use disorder. Readings such as the AA "Big Book," the NA "Basic Text," readings about specific substances (e.g., NIAAA and NIDA materials), and interactive workbooks and journals can be used to help clients address treatment issues in their ongoing recovery (see the Client Workbook; Daley 2004a, 2004b, 2005; Daley & Douaihy, 2005; www.staying sober.lifejournal.com).

11. *Coping Skills.* Learning coping skills to deal with problems resulting from or contributing to substance use disorders is critical for long-term success with clients. Clients often need help in developing cognitive, behavioral, and interpersonal skills to deal with a range of recovery challenges (e.g., managing cravings, upsetting feelings, interpersonal conflict, pressures to engage in substance use behavior, early warning signs of relapse—see Chapters 7 to 15) or managing co-occurring psychiatric disorders (see Chapters 16 and 17). Developing coping skills involves education, awareness, practice, and the ability to change ineffective coping responses. Coping is central to most cognitive-behavioral strategies, including relapse prevention responses (Daley & Marlatt, 2005; Marlatt & Donovan, 2005; Monti et al., 2002).

12. *Holistic Approach.* Treatment should reflect a consideration of the client's current and past pattern of substance use, medical and psychiatric condition, age, gender, family situation, ethnicity, and social environment. Clients with special needs (e.g., housing, vocational training, comorbid psychiatric illness) will need help

addressing these needs, particularly when they interfere with the process of recovery from a substance use disorder.

13. *Family Issues.* Since substance use disorders adversely affect the family, this issue should be discussed with the client. Focus can be on the impact of the substance use on the family, strategies to improve family communication and relationships, and what services can be of benefit to the family (e.g., professional and/or self-help). Involving the family is often helpful to both the client and the family (see Chapter 13). The client receives support from the family, and the family members get an opportunity to tell their story and receive help and support as well. When families are involved in treatment, especially with adolescents, the outcome improves (NIDA, 2003; Stanton & Heath, 2005; Stanton & Shadish, 1997).

14. *Social Networks.* A supportive social network facilitates recovery. Helping clients evaluate and develop social supports and participate in self-help programs plays a critical role in their long-term success (see Chapters 14 and 15). In some instances, clients will need help learning to identify possible sources of support and how to ask for help from others.

15. *Psychiatric Comorbidity.* Individuals with substance use disorders should be assessed for the possibility of a co-existing psychiatric disorder (see Chapter 16). If a psychiatric disorder exists, the treatment plan and clinical approaches used should take this into consideration (see Chapter 17). Clients with more severe types of psychiatric disorder may need "dual diagnosis enhanced" services, whereas those with less severe disorders can benefit from "dual diagnosis capable" services (ASAM, 2001). The former are usually provided in mental health systems, the latter in addiction medicine systems.

16. *Lapse and Relapse.* Although there is considerable evidence of the effectiveness of treatment for substance use disorders, lapses and relapses are common. Many clients do not experience a linear path in their recovery. Issues related to lapse or relapse need to be addressed to better prepare the client to cope with potential high-risk situations, and to minimize the adverse effects of a return to substance use (see Chapters 18 and 19).

17. *Measuring Progress.* There are a variety of ways to measure progress, including cessation or reduction of substance use, reduction of biopsychosocial problems caused or worsened by substance use, and improvement in any domain of functioning. Progress is not an "all or none" phenomenon and should be measured relative to a specific client's problems and treatment goals (see Chapter 21). Treatment outcome is influenced by client (e.g., severity of substance use, motivation, personal resources), treatment (e.g., appropriateness, type and length of treatment), and environmental variables (e.g., family and social supports).

Brief Interventions

According to the stepped-care model of substance abuse treatment, clients who are in the Precontemplation or Contemplation stage of change may benefit from a brief intervention provided by the therapist or other health professional. The brief intervention will ideally move the client forward into the Preparation and Action stage of change. Brief interventions are time-limited strategies that are particularly useful in high-volume healthcare practices in which the providers (e.g., primary healthcare physicians in general practice, or trauma center or emergency care counselors or medical staff) have limited time to spend with the client. Brief interventions have also been applied successfully with binge-drinking college students, persons arrested for driving under the influence, homeless adolescents, pregnant mothers, and a variety of other high-risk populations (Bien, Miller, & Tonigan, 1993; Marlatt, 1998, 2000; Marlatt & Witkiewitz, 2002). Most of these programs involve an initial counseling session lasting from 5 to 20 minutes, usually with a choice of treatment goals (harm reduction or abstinence). Intervention strategies may vary from nonconfrontational approaches (e.g., motivational interviewing) to more direct delivery of advice (e.g., providing direct feedback, advising the client to abstain or cut down and to agree on a plan of action). A brief intervention can have long-term effects for many clients who otherwise would reject a commitment to long-term treatment as the first step. The key components of brief interventions are summarized in the acronym FRAMES (Bien, Miller, & Toniga, 1993):

1. _Feedback:_ The caregiver provides the client with specific objective feedback about the diagnosis or problems assessed through clinical interviews, medical records, laboratory reports, and/or collateral data (e.g., from a family member). This feedback gives the client valuable information about the diagnosis, effects of the problems, and possible interactions among several problems that may lead the client to agree to accept a referral for specialized treatment. With substance use problems, feedback can incorporate any significant laboratory findings. Examples include high blood alcohol levels, elevated liver enzymes, related medical disorders that are caused or exacerbated by substance abuse, urinalysis results, and others. Other feedback items may include the assessment of withdrawal symptoms, changes in tolerance, and behaviors or problems associated with the substance use (e.g., family, legal, work). For example, the caregiver may say to a client, "Ms. Blake, our laboratory results show high levels of cocaine in your urine. Also, you and your husband both told us that you've been using large amounts of cocaine every day, you can't seem to stop for more than a few days at a time even though you want to, you feel depressed and suicidal when you run out of drugs, you're getting into arguments with your husband, you've missed a lot of work, and you've spent a lot of money on drugs. All of these symptoms and behaviors, taken together, show that you meet the criteria for cocaine dependence. You even said yourself that you were addicted, so you know there's a serious problem with your drug use. I also believe the anxiety and heart palpitations that you've told me about are probably caused by your drug use. The amount of cocaine that you are using and the frequency at which you use indicate a very serious level of addiction."

2. _Responsibility:_ The decision to seek help or change is the sole responsibility of the client. While recommendations can be provided about treatment programs or change strategies, the client must bear the responsibility for the disorder and for making the decision to engage in treatment. Specific and concrete feedback regarding the diagnosis and problems caused by the client's substance may instill guilt and motivate the client to take responsibility for seeking further help.

3. _Advice:_ The client is given specific advice on how to deal with his problem. For example, to the client who has a problem with alcohol, the physician might say, "We've seen other people like you who've had trouble controlling their drinking really benefit from professional treatment. I'd strongly advise you to get help and would like to recommend you see . . . or attend the program at . . ." Or, "You told me you're worried about your drinking and how it's affecting your health and family. I would recommend you stop drinking altogether, since there's a good chance your liver would return to normal, and you could also begin to work out your problems with your wife. I think you would benefit from treatment at . . ."

4. _Menu:_ Different treatment or change options are provided to the client, who chooses from among them. The evaluator might say to a client with moderate problem with marijuana or alcohol abuse, "I can help you address your concerns about marijuana (or alcohol) abuse." Or, for a more severe type of substance dependence the evaluator may say, "You describe a severe problem with heroin in which you've been injecting large amounts of the drug every day for almost 2 years. I would like to refer you for detoxification and a rehabilitation program. There are several good treatment programs in this area as well as outside of here. Let me tell you about them, and you can decide which one you think you would like to attend."

5. _Empathy:_ A positive therapeutic alliance or relationship with a client is built on empathy. This refers to the caregiver's ability to accept, understand, and have a sincere desire to help the client and to convey this to the client. While it is easy to take an empathic stance with a depressed client, it often is more difficult to feel empathy toward the client with an alcohol or other drug problem. Judgmentalism and negative attitudes or reactions will impede the ability to help these clients, so the physician or caregiver must be aware of personal attitudes, perceptions, and beliefs regarding these types of problems. If, for example, alcohol or other drug dependence is viewed as bad behavior and a flaw in the individual rather than a serious biopsychosocial disorder, the professional will

be less able to help the affected client. Healthcare and mental health professionals sometimes struggle with this issue because they view the addicted client as manipulative, unmotivated, antisocial, or a hassle to deal with. They judge the client based on the behavior shown. Rather than see the behavior as part of the addiction, which is amenable to change, some clinicians react negatively and push the client away. Accepting the client and conveying empathy are needed to influence the client to participate in treatment or change.

6. *Self-efficacy:* The caregiver supports the client's belief in the ability to make positive changes whenever possible. Realistic optimism that things can get better is conveyed. For example, the client may be told, "It sounds like you've succeeded in the past coping with your addiction when you had the support of your wife, saw a therapist regularly, and went to NA meetings. You're in a good position to do this again, which I think will help you get back on the recovery track." Or, "You've been very honest about how close you came to drinking again. The fact that you didn't drink, even though you wanted very badly to do so, is a good sign that you have both the desire and ability to stay sober. Let's talk more about other things that can help you stay sober and prevent a relapse."

Treatment Outcome

Many reviews and meta-analyses of the literature, as well as outcomes from specific multisite or single-site clinical trials of individual, group, family, pharmacologic, or combined treatments, document the positive outcome of clinical interventions (Crits-Cristoph et al., 1999; CSAT, 1999a, 1999c, 2000a; Daley & Marlatt, 2005; Higgins & Silverman, 1999; Hubbard, 2005; McLellan et al., 2000; NIAAA, 1999, 2000, 2005; NIDA, 2000a; Rounsaville, Carroll, & Back, 2005; Stanton & Heath, 2005). Treatment is effective to the extent that the client remains long enough to benefit from it.

While brief interventions of less than 90 days in active treatment are effective with alcohol use disorders, at the present time there is limited evidence that these brief interventions are effective with drug use disorders. The exception are motivational interventions that help the drug-abusing or -dependent individual engage in treatment or make a successful transition from one level of care to the next (e.g., inpatient or residential to outpatient care; Daley et al., 1998).

Positive effects of treatment from this vast literature include the following:

- Improved rates of engagement in treatment

- Improved rates of adherence to treatment

- Improved rates of treatment completion

- Cessation of substance use

- Reduction of the frequency and quantity of substances used

- Improved functioning—physical, psychological, financial, spiritual, and social (e.g., lower rates of HIV transmission or acquisition; lower rates of use of emergency room services; lower rates of suicidality)

- Improvement in family functioning and relationships to family members, and reduced rates of family break-ups due to separation, divorce, or losing children to child welfare protective services

- Increased marital satisfaction and stability

- Better outcomes for pregnant mothers (e.g., fewer children are born addicted; children are born at a higher weight and require less expensive specialized neonatal care)

- Improved social functioning—reduction in criminal behaviors or arrests for driving under the influence, increase in employment rates, and less dependence on welfare

Chapter 6 *Medications for Substance Use Problems*

(Corresponds to chapter 15 of the workbook)

Medications for Substance Dependence

Medications are used in several ways in the treatment of alcohol or drug dependence (O'Brien, 2005; Vocci, Acri, & Elkashef, 2005). First, they are used to attenuate withdrawal symptoms for individuals with a physiological dependence on alcohol or other drugs. Second, they are used as replacement medications for addictive substances such as heroin or nicotine. For example, methadone is given as maintenance therapy to some clients addicted to heroin or other opioids. This allows the addicted individual to transfer the addiction from a nonprescribed street drug to a medication provided under medical supervision. Third, medications may be used to reduce cravings for alcohol and drugs, and hence lower relapse risk. For example, naltrexone, acamprosate, and topiramate are used with alcoholics, and modafinil and baclofen are used with cocaine addicts. Fourth, drugs may serve another purpose with a specific type of addictive substance. For example, disulfiram is used with alcoholics as a deterrent to alcohol use, since drinking with this drug in the system creates an aversive reaction with the alcoholic. Naltrexone (Trexan) blocks the euphoric effects of opiate drugs so the addict who uses these drugs does not experience the usual euphoric effects of opioids. And last, medications are used to treat co-occurring psychiatric or medical disorders. Medications used to treat addiction are viewed as most effective when used with therapy or counseling (O'Brien, 2005).

Withdrawing From Addictive Drugs

If the client has a physical addiction to alcohol or other drugs and has been unable to quit on his or her own, or if the client has a history of complications related to withdrawal such as seizures, delirium tremens

(DTs), severe depression, or suicidal feelings, detoxification in a supervised environment is needed to reduce, stop, or prevent withdrawal symptoms. Less severe forms of dependency can be managed on an outpatient basis. The following sections describe withdrawal symptoms for various substances and the medications used to help clients withdraw from substances or to help clients in need of medication maintenance (ASAM, 2003; Galanter & Kleber, 2004; Garbutt et al., 1999; Kranzler & Jaffe, 2003; Ling et al., 1996; Lowinson et al., 2005; Schuckit, 2000).

Alcohol Withdrawal

Withdrawal symptoms usually start on the first day and peak on the second or third day after completely stopping or significantly cutting down alcohol use after drinking heavily for several days or longer. Symptoms include tremors of the hands, tongue, and eyelids; nausea and vomiting; weakness; sweating; elevated blood pressure or tachycardia; anxiety; depression or irritability; and low blood pressure when in an upright position. More severe cases of withdrawal may include delusions (false beliefs), hallucinations, seizures, or agitated behavior. Withdrawal usually takes several days and may involve taking depressant medications such as Valium, Librium, or Serax.

Depressant Withdrawal

Heavy or prolonged use of other depressant drugs such as sedatives and tranquilizers can cause withdrawal symptoms similar to alcohol withdrawal symptoms. Withdrawal from depressant drugs is done by gradually tapering the client off the drug he or she is addicted to, or by substituting a drug that is similar in its action on the central nervous system. Withdrawal from some of the longer-acting tranquilizers takes more than a few days. The process may start in an inpatient setting, and then continue in an outpatient setting.

Opiate or Narcotic Withdrawal

Symptoms of withdrawal from heavy, prolonged use of opiates or narcotics include runny nose, tearing eyes, dilated pupils, gooseflesh, sweating, diarrhea, yawning, mild hypertension, tachycardia, fever, and insomnia. Symptoms start 6 to 12 hours after the last drug dose, peak on the second or third day, and usually end within 7 to 14 days, depending on the specific opiate or narcotic used and length of the addiction. Withdrawal from heroin or other opiate or narcotic drugs involves taking methadone, buprenorphine, or clonidine.

Cocaine and Stimulant Withdrawal

Depressed mood, fatigue, disturbed sleep, and increased dreaming are symptoms associated with withdrawal from heavy, prolonged use of stimulant drugs. Although there are no severe physical withdrawal symptoms associated with addiction to cocaine or stimulant drugs, amantadine has been used to help addicted clients through the withdrawal process, with mixed results.

Nicotine Withdrawal

Symptoms of nicotine withdrawal usually begin within hours of stopping or significantly reducing tobacco use after heavy, regular use. These symptoms include tobacco cravings, irritability, anxiety, concentration problems, restlessness, headaches, drowsiness, and gastrointestinal disturbances. There are several medications approved by the U.S. Food and Drug Administration (FDA) to help addicted smokers stop smoking and remain abstinent (Schmitz & Delaune, 2005). These may be used singly or in combination. It is also recommended that medications be used with counseling. First-line medications used to help smokers increase long-term abstinence rates include bupropion SR (Zyban) and nicotine gum, inhalers, sprays, or patches. Second-line medications, not approved by the FDA, are sometimes used when first-line medications are ineffective or cannot be used due to pregnancy or breast-feeding. These include clonidine (Catapres) and nortriptyline (Pamelor).

Nicotine gum or patches can be used to help the client gradually withdraw from the use of tobacco products such as cigarettes. Nicotine gum helps to minimize nicotine withdrawal symptoms and to decrease the smoker's risk of relapse in the early weeks and months of being tobacco-free. However, it can be addictive and should not be used if the client has certain medical conditions such as a recent myocardial infarction, vasospastic disease, cardiac arrhythmia, esophagitis, peptic ulcers, or inflammation of the mouth or throat. Some people complain of side effects such as hiccups, nausea, jaw irritation, and bad taste. A nicotine patch can help stop withdrawal symptoms by decreasing tension, anxiety, irritability, restlessness, and nicotine cravings. The patch gradually releases nicotine into the system, usually over a period of 24 hours. Patches can be used up to several weeks or longer.

Nicotine nasal sprays and nicotine inhalers decrease the urge to smoke. Nicotine replacement allows the client to deal with the psychological, social, and behavioral aspects of the nicotine habit without having to simultaneously deal with the physical addiction. Medications are most effective when used in conjunction with a behavior change program.

Case Example: Lorraine (Nicotine Patch)

Lorraine is a 59-year-old teacher with a 35-year history of dependence on cigarettes. She had quit smoking on her own many times but always relapsed within several weeks. Lorraine was smoking nearly three packs a day when she decided to try a nicotine patch rather than quit cold turkey. Over the course of a month, Lorraine was able to stop cigarettes completely and has been smoke-free for 9 months. She reports occasional cravings but feels she's able to talk herself out of wanting to smoke. Lorraine also exercises regularly and has learned ways of reducing stress in her life to decrease the likelihood of smoking to cope with stress.

Abstinence From Alcohol

Disulfiram (trade name Antabuse) is a drug used by some clients to help "buy time" when they want to drink. Antabuse stays in the system for a week or longer, so if the client decides to drink, he or she has to wait for Antabuse to clear the system to avoid getting sick. If the client ingests any alcohol while Antabuse is in his or her system, the client will get sick because Antabuse interrupts the body's normal process of metabolizing alcohol. The idea behind this drug is simple: it will ideally deter the client from using any alcohol, but if the client does drink and get sick, the negative reinforcement will deter him or her from drinking in the future. Antabuse usually is recommended only for short-term use (6 months or less) due to its effects on the liver. Also, a fatal reaction between alcohol and Antabuse can occur, so it is not recommended for the impulsive client.

Naltrexone (trade name ReVia) was initially developed for use with people addicted to heroin or other opiate drugs, with the objective of blocking the euphoric effects of these drugs. More recently, this medication has been used with alcoholics. ReVia appears to block the effects of the body's own opioids, which reduces the reinforcing properties of alcohol and thus the desire to drink. ReVia cannot be used if the client is currently using any narcotic drugs or if he or she has hepatitis or liver disease.

A newer medication used extensively in Europe and approved by the FDA for use in the United States in 2004 is acamprosate (trade name Campral). Results from multiple studies and a meta-analysis of 17 clinical trials shows that this medication increases the proportion of alcohol-dependent individuals who maintain abstinence from alcohol (NIAAA, 2005).

Case Example: Christina (Naltrexone)

■ *Christina is a 38-year-old with a very long history of alcohol dependence. Although she had been in numerous treatment programs and had participated in AA meetings, the longest she had ever been sober was 5 weeks. Christina returned to outpatient treatment as a result of a DWI charge. Given her strong cravings for alcohol and inability to stay sober with other treatments, Christina agreed to use naltrexone and attend therapy sessions twice per week. She has now been sober for over 7 months and strongly believes that ReVia (naltrexone) has helped her recover. Christina has also been able to decrease the frequency of her therapy sessions.* ▪

Abstinence From Opiates

Drugs such as Trexan or LAAM are opiate antagonists that block the euphoric effects of heroin or other opiate drugs. This type of drug reduces the client's desire to continue using opiates.

Some clients who are dependent on heroin or other opiate drugs have an extremely difficult time staying drug-free, even after participating in rehabilitation or other treatment programs. Methadone maintenance (MM) is a treatment in which use of the opiate drug is stopped and methadone, a longer-acting opiate, is substituted. MM works best in combination with counseling or therapy. Regular doses of methadone help the addicted person avoid using opiate drugs. Very importantly, MM, when combined with counseling, enables the addicted person to resume normal life activities such as work. Although it is intended as an interim treatment of a few months to a year or two, some clients continue to use MM for many years. Methadone can be given only at specially licensed clinics. Both public and private MM clinics are available.

Buprenorphine (trade names Buprenex, Suboxone, and Subutex) is a partial agonist developed as an effective alternative to methadone or LAAM. This drug can precipitate or suppress opiate withdrawal symptoms and help the opiate addict maintain abstinence from other opioids such as heroin. It is safer than methadone or LAAM in regard to drug-induced respiratory depression (Fundala & O'Brien, 2005). Buprenorphine can be prescribed by certified physicians in their offices as well as licensed narcotic addiction treatment programs.

Case Example: Patrick (Methadone Maintenance)

Patrick is a 34-year-old nurse whose addiction to heroin has caused him to lose a marriage, get fired from one job, and experience numerous other legal, emotional, and financial problems. Although he had been detoxified and had participated in several rehabilitation programs, outpatient therapy, and NA, he was unable to stay drug-free for longer than a few months until he got in a methadone maintenance program. Patrick has not used heroin or any other drugs or alcohol in almost 2 years. He has been able to return to gainful employment and feels his life is much improved. Talking about daily hassles and stresses with his MM counselor helps Patrick keep from using alcohol or other drugs.

Abstinence From Cocaine and Other Stimulants

Stopping cocaine use does not always cause withdrawal symptoms. However, some individuals experience depression, anhedonia, sleep problems, increased appetite, psychomotor retardation, anxiety, and strong drug cravings (APA, 2000a). Over 40 different medications have been studied in the treatment of cocaine and other stimulant addiction, most in uncontrolled clinical trials. These include dopaminergic agonists that mimic cocaine effects (e.g., amphetamine, methylphenidate, pemoline), cocaine antagonists that block cocaine effects (e.g., bupropion, mazindol), medications that decrease cocaine reinforcements (e.g., SSRI antidepressants, disulfiram, carbamazepine, baclofen, and gabapentin), and a cocaine vaccine (Kosten & Sofuoglu, 2005). Medications with the most promise for use with cocaine addiction to reduce cravings or relapse risk are disulfiram, modafinil, topiramate, propranolol, and baclofen (O'Brien, 2005).

Medications for Co-existing Psychiatric Disorder

If the client has a psychiatric disorder in addition to the substance use disorder, he or she may benefit from the use of medications (Cornelius et al., 1997; CSAT, 2005a; Daley & Moss, 2002; Daley & Thase, 2004; Drake et al., 1998; Kupfer et al., 1992; Sammons & Schmidt, 2001). Psychiatric medications such as antidepressants sometimes have the added benefit of reducing the client's desire to use substances such as alcohol. However, some psychiatric medications, such as tranquilizers and sedatives, can be addictive and contribute to relapse (see Chapters 16 and 17 for a discussion of assessment and treatment of co-occurring psychiatric disorders).

Case Example: BJ (Mood Stabilizer)

BJ is a 46-year-old laborer with a long history of abuse of and dependence on alcohol, marijuana, and crack cocaine. His addiction has led to many problems and has played a major role in a long string of fights with other men. However, even in the absence of substance use, BJ is a violent man. After being sober for almost 2 months, he continued to experience severe mood swings with intense anger and irritability. These mood swings had always led him back to alcohol or drug use in the past. BJ was diagnosed with a mood disorder and reluctantly agreed to take Depakote, a mood stabilizer. To his surprise, he felt much better and did not impulsively return to drug use as he had in the past. For the first time in his life, BJ has been sober from both alcohol and drugs for over a year. He also reports that he hasn't been in any fights since starting the medication, and he feels his irritability and bad temper are now under control.

Medications as Adjunctive Versus Primary Treatments

For ongoing recovery from alcohol or other drug problems, medications should be used in conjunction with therapy, counseling, or participation in self-help programs. The amount of time medications should be taken depends on the particular client's history of substance use, problems caused by it, and response to prior treatment.

How to Know If the Client Needs Medication

Medications can help when the client in recovery:

- Has been unable to stay off alcohol, tobacco, or other drugs for longer than a few months at a time

- Has tried other forms of treatment and relapsed to using alcohol, tobacco, or other drugs

- Feels it is very difficult not to drink or use tobacco or other drugs, despite knowing he or she should quit and wanting to quit

- Often feels overwhelmed by cravings and strong desires to use alcohol, tobacco, or other drugs

- Has a lot to lose if he or she relapses, such as an important relationship, a job, or professional status or license

- Has his or her physical health or mental stability increasingly affected by the substance use the longer use continues

- Believes his or her life would be better if he or she stayed sober from alcohol, tobacco, or other drugs

- Believes medications will help him or her benefit more from other forms of treatment, such as professional therapy or participation in self-help groups

Sometimes questions are raised about the risks and side effects of medications. A cost-benefit analysis can help the client see the risks and benefits. Usually, the risks and costs of taking medications are small in comparison with the risks of continued dependency on alcohol, tobacco, or other drugs.

Change Issues and Strategies

Chapter 7   *Stages of Change and Using Therapy or Counseling*

(Corresponds to chapters 5 and 6 of the workbook)

Materials Needed

- Assessing Your Stage of Change Worksheet

- Decision-Making Matrix

- Completed Harmful Effects Worksheet from Chapter 3 of Workbook

- Therapy-Sabotaging Behavior Worksheet

Objectives

- To introduce the client to the concept of stages of change

- To help the client identify his or her current stage of change and issues to address in recovery

- To review strategies to help the client deal with low motivation

- To identify therapy-sabotaging behaviors and positive coping strategies

Introduction

Clients go through different stages when they stop using substances and make personal and lifestyle changes. Whereas some clients struggle with their recovery and never progress much beyond the first stage or two, others move more easily into more advanced stages and are able to explore intrapersonal and interpersonal issues that go beyond simply staying substance-free. There are several different conceptualizations of stages of change; the interested reader is encouraged to explore these by consulting the list of References and Suggested Readings. The authors find it helpful to use the paradigm of Prochaska, Norcross, and DiClemente (1994), which presents six stages of change: precontemplation, contemplation, preparation, action, maintenance, and termination:

1. The first stage of changing a substance problem, called *precontemplation*, is one in which the client isn't aware of a problem and is resistant to change. The client may be in denial and not see the alcohol or drug problem, even if other people can.

2. The second stage is called *contemplation*. During this stage the client acknowledges that he or she has a problem with alcohol or drugs and plans to take action within the next 6 months or so.

3. *Preparation* is the next stage. Here, the client plans within the next month to take some action regarding the alcohol or drug problem. The client usually lets others know about the change he or she is going to make. Even though the client wants to change, he or she still has mixed feelings about it: the client does and doesn't want to quit using alcohol or drugs. The client begins to think about the advantages of change.

4. The next stage, *action*, involves actually changing the alcohol or drug problem. The client makes a commitment to stop drinking alcohol, smoking, or using drugs. The commitment could be realized through self-change, a self-help group, or professional treatment. In addition to getting sober or clean, the client begins to learn more about how to change thinking, emotions, self-image, and behavior. The client learns that coping with a substance use problem requires a lot more than simply stopping the use. He or she addresses the "nuts and bolts" issues of recovery such as coping with thoughts and cravings for substances; being aware of people, places, and things that can influence him or her to use again; coping with upsetting feelings; and dealing with family and relationship problems. The client may become involved in self-help groups or other forms of social support and build structure into his or her life to reduce boredom.

5. *Maintenance*, or relapse prevention, is the next stage of change. During this stage, the client continues to make positive changes in himself or herself and in his or her lifestyle. The client works hard to prevent a return to alcohol or drug use and accepts that there are no easy or quick solutions to a substance use problem. The client learns to identify and manage relapse warning signs and high-risk situations. He or she works on balancing the various areas of life to improve his or her self-image. Many people stay in this stage for several years and find it helpful to participate in on-going recovery programs that help them maintain vigilance about relapse warning signs. This is why it isn't unusual for some people to attend support groups like AA or NA throughout their lives.

6. The final stage of change is called *termination*. In this stage, the substance use problem no longer presents a temptation or threat. The client's previous behavior doesn't return, and he or she has the confidence and skills to cope with life problems so that relapse is not very likely.

Recovery is seldom a smooth or linear process; clients may move back and forth between stages as their condition changes. Clients may revisit issues from early stages while dealing with issues in a later stage of recovery. For example, a client who has been abstinent for a significant period, is well grounded in recovery, and is working on changing interpersonal style to have more satisfying relationships could temporarily experience strong cravings and pressures to drink alcohol. Another client may have a lapse or relapse, requiring that the focus shift to re-establishing abstinence.

Major Points and Issues for Discussion

The following are major points and issues for discussion:

1. The therapist discusses the concept of stages of change and helps the client become aware that recovery is not a linear process in which he or she will move smoothly from one stage to the next. The stages are general guidelines to help the client know what to expect during the recovery process. The time a client spends in a specific recovery stage is individual and depends on his or her

unique situation, motivation to change, social supports, and capability to change.

2.   The therapist helps the client determine which stage of recovery he or she is in by having the client complete the Assessing Your Stage of Change Worksheet in Chapter 5 of the Workbook.

3.   The therapist helps the client address motivational struggles during recovery by using any of the following strategies:

   ▪ The client reviews the reasons for quitting substance use and identifies short-term and long-term benefits. The client completes the Decision-Making Matrix in Chapter 5 of the Workbook, which lists short-term and long-term consequences (positive and negative) of stopping or continuing substance use.

   ▪ The client reviews the problems caused or worsened by substance use and identifies problems that might occur if he or she continues to use alcohol or other drugs. The client reviews his or her completed Harmful Effects Worksheet to identify problems in functioning that are associated with the substance use.

   ▪ The client can think about specific adverse effects of substance use on important people such as family members (e.g., spouse, children).

   ▪ The client can remind himself or herself that motivational crises usually pass in time and that sticking with the recovery program is the best way to lower relapse potential.

   ▪ The client can seek help or guidance from the therapist, peers in recovery, or supportive friends and family.

   ▪ The client can pray or meditate.

4.   Some clients will need help in facing their reluctance to examine ways in which their substance use problem adversely affects others. Clients involved in a 12-step program can be encouraged to learn about the "making amends" steps (steps 8 and 9) that can help them undo some of the damage caused to others. Clients who make amends should be prepared for the possibility that other people may not respond favorably. Clients sometimes experience anger, hostility, and rejection when they attempt to make amends with a family member, friend, or colleague. The client who antici-

Decision-Making Matrix: Pros and Cons of Quitting

Instructions: In the sections below, write the pros and cons of quitting and of continuing to use alcohol, tobacco, or other drugs. Provide examples of both immediate and long-term consequences of each decision.

To stop using or remain abstinent

Immediate consequences		Long-term consequences	
Positive	**Negative**	**Positive**	**Negative**
Better sleep	Bored	Better health	Need to have new
Fewer family arguments	Cravings are strong	Happier family life	fun activities
Save money	Hard to be around	Won't lose job	
No hangovers	drinking buddies	Much better	
Won't feel guilty	Frustration	financial condition	
	Denial of pleasure		

To continue using

Immediate consequences		Long-term consequences	
Positive	**Negative**	**Positive**	**Negative**
Relaxes me	Wife upset	Always an easy way	Health problems
It's familiar	Costs a lot	to escape reality or	Could lose job
Fit in with friends	Lost time at work	unpleasant feelings	Family frustration with
	Feel guilty		me will increase
			Could lose family and
			friends
			Hate myself

Figure 7.1

Example of a completed Decision-Making Matrix.

pates and prepares for others' adverse reactions will be better able to cope should these actually occur. This preparation may require changing negative interpretations of rejection or anger so that it is not taken personally. Some interpersonal relationships will have been harmed so much that the client's attempts to make amends will never be accepted.

5. The therapist should introduce the client to therapy-sabotaging behaviors. These are attitudes and behaviors that decrease the likelihood of positive change or appropriate use of therapy. A few examples are (a) not attending therapy sessions on time, or missing them; (b) not following through and completing recovery assignments or journal exercises between therapy sessions; and (c) not opening up and sharing thoughts, feelings, or problems with the therapist. If a client has previously participated in treatment, the therapist should have him or her complete the Therapy-Sabotaging Behavior Worksheet (Figure 7.2). The therapist and client can use the client's answers to collaboratively develop strategies to minimize and cope with such behaviors should they occur in the future.

6. As the client progresses through recovery and establishes a foundation of abstinence, he or she will become more able to face emotional issues from the past, examine personality issues (often referred to as "character defects" in 12-step programs), and focus on broader issues such as how and why to work toward a balanced lifestyle.

7. In all stages of recovery, clients face the possibility of lapse and relapse. Any lapse or relapse should be discussed with the therapist, and can also be discussed with members of the client's recovery support system.

Homework for Client

- Complete the Assessing Your Stage of Change Worksheet.
- Review the Harmful Effects Worksheet completed in Chapter 3.
- Complete the Decision-Making Matrix.
- Complete the Therapy-Sabotaging Behavior Worksheet.
- Complete the Past Treatment Exercises Worksheet.

Therapy-Sabotaging Behavior Worksheet

Instructions: Review each behavior below. Place a check mark (√) next to it if you've ever experienced it in relation to your therapy or counseling. Then, choose two behaviors you have experienced and develop an action plan for coping with each behavior.

√ Not attending my sessions on time
___ Skipping my session entirely
___ Missing sessions because I was upset with my counselor
___ Dropping out of counseling after only a few sessions
√ Not following through and completing assignments or journal exercises between my counseling sessions
___ Blaming my counselor for not helping me enough
___ Talking about how to change in my sessions but not actually translating these changes into my life
___ Expecting my counselor to tell me what to talk about in my sessions
___ Not opening up and telling my counselor what I really think or feel

___ Not telling my counselor when I feel like using substances or have actually used between sessions
___ Constantly calling my counselor on the phone or leaving messages
___ Placing unrealistic demands on my counselor
___ Not properly taking medications such as Antabuse or naltrexone, or medications for a concurrent psychiatric disorder
___ Not accepting responsibility for those things over which I have control
___ Not accepting responsibility for _____ (things over which I have influence)
___ Blaming others for my behavior choices
___ Placing myself in high-risk situations

Behavior 1: Not attending sessions on time

Action Plan: Figure out why I'm late for my sessions and other things in my life; think about my sessions as being scheduled a half-hour before the actual time; remind myself that I'm the one who misses out if I get less time for counseling; and make an agreement with my therapist that I will show up on time.

Behavior 2: Not following through and completing the assignments or journal exercises between my counseling sessions.

Action Plan: Both this problem and the one above seem to relate to my problem of being responsible. I've got to change my attitude and constantly tell myself that doing what I'm supposed to do is for my own good; challenge my poor excuses that I "forget" to do my assignments; and set time aside each week to carefully review and complete my assignment.

Figure 7.2

Example of a completed Therapy-Sabotaging Behavior Worksheet.

Chapter 8 | *Goal Planning in Recovery*

(Corresponds to chapter 7 of the workbook)

Materials Needed

- Goal Planning Worksheet

Objectives

- To help the client learn about the various domains of functioning related to recovery

- To help the client identify specific recovery goals related to the various domains of functioning

- To help the client develop strategies to reach his or her identified goals

Introduction

Recovery is a process of managing the substance use disorder and changing oneself. Recovery may address any domain of the client's functioning: physical, emotional or psychological, family, social or interpersonal, spiritual, or lifestyle. The goals a particular client chooses and his or her ability to meet these goals depend on the client's stage of recovery as well as several other factors:

- Severity of the substance use and problems caused by it

- Motivation to change

- Internal psychological resources (e.g., insight, resilience, capacity for tolerating distress, ability to work toward long-term goals and delay gratification)

■ Interpersonal relationships and external support system

■ Presence of comorbidity (medical, psychiatric, social)

Recovery involves making changes and developing specific skills to deal with the problems and demands of being substance-free. Following is a review of some of the changes that clients may wish to make in each major domain of functioning:

■ *Physical.* Take care of medical or dental problems; improve diet; lose weight; practice stress reduction; exercise; and learn to cope with physical cravings to use substances.

■ *Emotional or psychological.* Accept the substance use disorder; change negative or distorted thinking or beliefs; improve ability to cope with stress, problems in life, or upsetting feelings; address coexisting psychiatric disorders; and deal with past psychological trauma.

■ *Family.* Involve the family in the recovery process, assess the impact of substance use on the family, make amends for harm caused to family, and work with the family to improve communication and interactions.

■ *Social or interpersonal.* Establish relationships with sober people; participate in enjoyable leisure activities that do not involve substance use; learn to refuse offers to use substances; address interpersonal conflicts or problems; and deal with legal, financial, work, or academic problems caused by substance use.

■ *Spiritual.* Deal with guilt and shame issues; develop meaning in life; rely on God or a higher power; and explore other personal aspects of spiritual growth.

Major Points and Issues for Discussion

The following are major points and issues for discussion:

1. The therapist and client discuss the recovery process and different domains of recovery: physical, emotional or psychological, family, social or interpersonal, spiritual and lifestyle.

2. The therapist and client discuss the client's main goal in relation to substance use. Although many clients will choose total abstinence as their initial goal, some may choose a reduction in use. For example, not all clients with an alcohol problem will be physically or psychologically dependent on alcohol or suffer numerous adverse effects from drinking. Some of these clients may wish to drink less alcohol so that drinking does not cause any harm in their lives.

3. The therapist determines if reduction of substance use is realistic for the client who chooses this goal. If the client has a history of substance dependence, suffers many adverse effects of substance use, has a significant concurrent medical or psychiatric problem, or may suffer a major loss if substances are used (e.g., clients who are mandated to abstain by court or employer), reduction of use is not a realistic goal. The client will ultimately choose the goal that he or she wants over the goal that the therapist wants. However, if the therapist strongly feels that total abstinence is the most appropriate goal, he or she should share this position with the client and give a rationale.

4. The therapist helps the client prioritize recovery goals and provides feedback regarding the client's goals and proposed strategies to achieve these goals. The client should understand the importance of having both short-term and long-term goals. Goals provide a measuring stick by which progress can be evaluated. The client should complete the Goal-Planning Worksheet (Figure 8.1) to guide him or her in the process of identifying goals and developing an action plan to achieve these goals.

5. It is preferable for the therapist to move the client toward finding his or her own strategies for dealing with a specific problem or recovery issue. However, the therapist can provide additional suggestions when appropriate. It is helpful in the early stages of recovery for the therapist to give direct suggestions, especially when the client is struggling with a particular issue or problem that threatens his or her sobriety, such as persistent cravings, periods of low motivation, or pressure from a significant other to use substances.

Goal Planning Worksheet

Instructions: For each domain of recovery, list any changes you want to make. For each change that you identify, write the steps you can take to help you achieve your goal. Try to be as concrete as you can in identifying your goals and your change strategies.

Change	Goal	Steps toward change
Physical	Lose 20 pounds.	Start a regular exercise program; change diet to reduce calories taken in; greatly reduce amount of sweets I eat; don't keep cakes and pies in my house.
Emotional or phychological	Learn to control angry impulses.	Catch myself early when I'm mad so I don't let things build up; learn to put my feelings into words; figure out if things are really worth getting mad about; walk away if I feel like getting physical with someone else.
Family	Gain the trust of my family back. A better relationship with my kids.	Accept that I have to be patient with my family; invite them to attend counseling sessions with me; spend time with my kids; take an active role in their lives by being interested in what they say and do; attend my kids' sports and school events.
Social or interpersonal	Improve relationship with Jason.	Invite him over for dinner; apologize for taking advantage of him when I was drinking and explain that I'm working at sobriety; offer to help him.
Spiritual	Reduce guilty feelings about myself and empty feeling.	Share feelings in therapy and group meetings; pray; return to regular church services.
Other (work, economic, etc.)	Reduce debt and save money for emergencies.	Prioritize my debts; make and follow a budget; have $50 taken out of each paycheck for my savings account.

Figure 8.1

Example of a completed Goal Planning Worksheet.

6. When working with the client on a specific problem or recovery issue, the therapist should assess the client's coping skills to determine if he or she needs additional help in learning specific skills to manage a particular problem. For example, knowing that a client has inadequate coping skills and is at high risk to act out angry feelings through violence or substance use can help the therapist devise interventions to address this specific deficit.

7. In helping the client to improve or develop new coping skills, the therapist should focus on cognitive, behavioral, and interpersonal strategies so that the client is exposed to a variety of approaches to dealing with problems. For example, improving relationships may require a client to alter beliefs regarding reciprocity or self-disclosure, learn to act more assertively, or learn to be more empathetic toward others.

8. If the client is unable to meet a particular goal, the therapist should help him or her figure out what is getting in the way. Is the goal too ambitious or unrealistic? Does the client have adequate internal or external resources to help him or her reach the goal? Are there significant people who are sabotaging the client's effort to reach the goal?

Homework for Client

▓ Complete the Goal-Planning Worksheet.

Chapter 9   *Managing Cravings and Urges to Use Substances*

(Corresponds to chapter 8 of the workbook)

Materials Needed

- Daily Craving Record
- Substance Use Triggers Worksheet

Objectives

- To help the client define and label a craving to use substances
- To teach the client to monitor and track cravings over time, and to rate the level of intensity of cravings
- To identify internal and external factors that trigger cravings
- To help the client learn cognitive, behavioral, environmental, and interpersonal strategies to manage cravings

Introduction

A craving or longing for alcohol, tobacco, or other drugs is very common, especially in the early weeks and months of stopping substance use, regardless of how motivated clients are to stay substance-free. Cravings are mediated by brain activation in the amygdala region. Cravings can be activated by exposure to drug cues via classical conditioning. An urge is the client's intention to use alcohol or drugs once he or she experiences a craving. Usually, cravings decrease in frequency and intensity as recovery progresses and the client abstains from substance use. The client may be surprised by how strong a craving can be and how it can increase positive thoughts about the effects of a substance. The client who is overcoming a physical addiction is especially vulnerable to cravings during the first days and weeks of abstinence. Some clients report an overwhelming compulsion to use substances when they first stop using, even after completing the acute withdrawal process, a condition influenced by changes in brain neurochemistry, psychological coping mechanisms, and the social environment.

External factors trigger cravings. External factors include people with whom the client associated while drinking or using drugs; places or events where substances were used; and situations in which alcohol, tobacco, or other drugs were available. Many environmental cues trigger cravings: food; coffee; the sigh or smell of alcohol or drugs; ads for liquor or tobacco products; cigarette machines; tobacco shops; driving by a bar or club where the client used to drink; needles, mirrors, pipes, papers, or other drug paraphernalia; and music associated with partying, money, paychecks, or sex. The list of environmental cues is endless. In addition to common ones mentioned above, there are many cues unique to each person in recovery.

Internal factors trigger cravings as well. Internal factors include feelings such as anger, anxiety, boredom, depression, or frustration; physical pain or symptoms; and positive memories or thoughts of using substances. Physical withdrawal symptoms are very powerful triggers during the early stages of stopping substance use.

The intensity of a craving can vary from mild to extremely strong and powerful. Some clients report feeling overwhelmed and tortured by cravings when they first initiate recovery. It takes time for their bodies to adjust to being substance-free and for them to learn practical ways of managing cravings. The risk of relapse increases for clients who are unable to identify cravings and implement coping strategies.

Major Points and Issues for Discussion

The following are major points and issues for discussion:

1. The therapist helps the client identify cravings as the first step to managing them. The client needs to know how cravings are mani-

fested in physical and mental symptoms and behaviors. Cravings may show in anxiety; restlessness; stomach distress; excessive energy; inability to sit still; irritability; or thoughts, fantasies, and dreams of using. They may be overt and out of the client's immediate awareness.

2. The therapist informs the client that cravings to use alcohol, tobacco, or other drugs are very common after one stops using, especially in the first few weeks or months of recovery. Cravings can be experienced regardless of how motivated a client is to stay substance-free; therefore, being able to identify and label cravings is necessary for recovery to progress.

3. The client completes the Daily Craving Record (Figure 9.1) for several weeks or months to monitor and rate cravings during the early phases of recovery. Daily rating help the client to remain vigilant and to see how cravings wax and wane over time. The severity of cravings often declines as recovery progresses. Certain patterns may emerge as the client rates cravings regularly. For example, a client may become aware that cravings are more intense during certain times or days of the week. As shown in Figure 9.1, Sharon's daily rating were severe for the first 2 to 3 weeks and moderate to severe during the next 2 to 3 weeks. The intensity of her cravings decreased during months 2 and 3. About 6 weeks into her abstinence (November 16), she experienced severe cravings for a day. Recently, her cravings have increased. Sharon has been able to identify a connection between upset feelings in a relationship and an increase in the severity of cravings.

4. Identifying the client's weakest and strongest periods of cravings and urges since the last session and processing what was different between these periods can help the client learn what contributes to more difficult periods. The in turn can lead to discussions on how to manage times during which cravings and urges are the strongest and the client feels most vulnerable.

5. Cravings can take on a life of their own and exert a great influence on the client's thinking and actions. For example, reactions to an intense craving can lead to relapse if the client goes into a bar to socialize or attends a party where alcohol or drugs are readily available.

Daily Craving Record

Ratings of Intensity of Cravings

Instructions: Each day, use the scale to rate the average intensity (0–5) of your cravings to use alcohol, tobacco, or other drugs.

	0	1	2	3	4	5
	None	Low		Moderate		Severe

Month: October

Day	1	2	3	4	5	6	7	8	9	10	11	12	13	14	15	16
Rating	5	5	4	4	5	5	4	4	5	4	4	3	4	4	5	4
Day	17	18	19	20	21	22	23	24	25	26	27	28	29	30	31	
Rating	4	3	3	3	4	3	3	5	3	3	3	3	2	3	3	

Month: November

Day	1	2	3	4	5	6	7	8	9	10	11	12	13	14	15	16
Rating	3	3	2	4	3	3	3	2	2	3	3	3	3	3	3	5
Day	17	18	19	20	21	22	23	24	25	26	27	28	29	30	31	
Rating	3	2	3	3	3	3	2	2	3	2	3	3	3	3		

Month: December

Day	1	2	3	4	5	6	7	8	9	10	11	12	13	14	15	16
Rating	3	2	2	3	3	2	2	1	2	2	2	2	2	3	2	1
Day	17	18	19	20	21	22	23	24	25	26	27	28	29	30	31	
Rating	1	2	2	1	2	2	2	2	2							

Figure 9.1

Example of a completed Daily Craving Record.

6. The therapist emphasizes the importance of identifying both external and internal factors that trigger cravings. The client should complete the Substance Use Triggers Worksheet (Figure 9.2). This worksheet can be used to identify external triggers such as people, places, events, or situations that directly or indirectly affect the client's desire to use substances. The worksheet can also be used to identify internal triggers such as thoughts, feelings, memories, times of day, fantasies, dreams, and physical sensations. The client should look for not only obvious triggers, but also ones that may be more subtle but just as influential. The therapist can help the client rate the degree of threat of each trigger and deal first with the highest-rated triggers, as these represent the greatest relapse risk.

7. The therapist reviews the client's coping strategies to help determine their potential usefulness. The therapist should try to ensure that the client has a variety of strategies to manage cravings and that the strategies discussed are related to the client's situation.

8. The therapist reviews environmental coping strategies such as (a) reducing environmental cues by getting rid of substances the client is trying to quit and (b) getting rid of paraphernalia associated with preparing or using substances such as lighters, ashtrays, needles, mirrors, pipes, and papers.

9. The therapist reviews cognitive coping strategies such as (a) learning to talk oneself out of using when one craves alcohol, tobacco, or other drugs; (b) reminding oneself that cravings are temporary and will pass in time; (c) putting off responding to the craving for a while to buy time; (d) remembering the negative aspects of substance use and the positive aspects of not using; (e) reminding oneself that cravings are usually triggered by external cues, not by willpower failure, and that just because one experiences a craving does not mean that one has to give in to the urge—one can accept craving as a natural conditioning reaction; and (f) meditating or asking for help through prayer or personal dialogue with God or a higher power.

10. The therapist reviews behavioral coping strategies such as (a) avoiding or escaping high-risk situations and finding alternative activities; (b) distracting oneself through involvement in an activity unrelated

Substance Use Triggers Worksheet

Instructions: List people, places, events, situations, objects, feelings, thoughts, memories, or times of day that trigger your cravings or urges. Rate the level of threat presented by each trigger using the scale below. Finally, list strategies for coping with each trigger that will help you avoid using.

0 —————— 1 —————— 2 —————— 3 —————— 4 —————— 5

No Threat   Moderate Threat   Severe Threat

Trigger (external or internal)	Level of threat (0–5)	Coping strategies
Drug dealer	5	Avoid him; don't talk on phone when he calls.
Guys I got high with	5	Stop going to parties or socializing where drugs are used; limit contact to non-drug use activities; avoid some guys completely.
Brother and his apartment	3	Let him know I quit using and ask him not to offer me drugs or use around me; have visits with him at my place.
Angry after arguing with girlfriend	4	Stop using this as an excuse to get high; learn to accept that it's OK to get mad without using for revenge or to "show her."
Feeling bored	4	Accept that my boredom will pass; have a list of activities to keep me occupied when boredom gets the best of me; take up some new hobbies; remind myself I can have fun without using drugs or being with others at parties who are getting high.
Pipes, mirrors	3	Get rid of my drug paraphernalia.

Figure 9.2

Example of a completed Substance Use Triggers Worksheet.

Instructions: List people, places, events, situations, objects, feelings, thoughts, memories, or times of day that trigger your cravings or urges. Rate the level of threat presented by each trigger using the scale below. Finally, list strategies for coping with each trigger that will help you avoid using.

```
0 ——————— 1 ——————— 2 ——————— 3 ——————— 4 ——————— 5
```

No Threat   Moderate Threat   Severe Threat

Trigger (external or internal)	Level of threat (0–5)	Coping strategies
Feeling tense and stressed out	4	Practice relaxation techniques; go for walks every day to reduce stress; tell myself I can decompress without a drink or a cigarette.
Coffee in the morning and after dinner	5	Review my reasons for quitting tobacco each morning; pray for strength to not smoke; use dessert coffees after dinner as the desire to smoke is not as great; go for walk with husband after dinner.
Break time at work	4	Change my routine at work during breaks and spend time with the non-smokers; replace cigarettes with gum and mints; and read a magazine during break.
Cocktail hour after work	3	Avoid going to bars after work; have non-alcohol drinks at home after work; ask husband not to drink alcohol in front of me and to have discussion of how our day went; play soothing music before dinner.
Feeling like I deserve a reward (alcohol) after a hard week of work	4	Find other rewards (buy self something nice, go to movie, go out to dinner and movie with husband).
Stressful visit with parents, especially when Dad gets drunk	5	Let parents know I won't stay for visits when Dad drinks; ask Mother to visit at our home if Dad refuses to not drink; ask my husband for support and talk about my upset feelings.
Getting stuck in traffic	3	Play tapes of favorite albums; listen to talk radio; refuse to let myself get frustrated; tell myself "I don't need a cigarette to get through traffic."

Figure 9.2 *continued*

to substance use; (c) engaging in physical exercise or activities to release tension; (d) writing in a journal or filling in the Daily Craving Record; and (e) reading recovery literature for information or inspiration. The therapist reviews interpersonal coping strategies such as (a) talking to other people in recovery and (b) talking to friends or family members.

11. The therapist reviews pharmacologic strategies that may help to ameliorate cravings for specific substances. Specific medications are discussed in Chapter 6.

12. Clients need encouragement and support in learning, practicing, and implementing coping skills. Although many clients learn these skills easily on an intellectual level, they frequently struggle to implement them in their daily lives. This is why regular practice and active use of coping skills is so important.

13. When the client reports that he or she has been able to cope with cravings, the therapist should provide reinforcement and help identify which specific strategies were used.

14. It is useful to start each therapy session with a "craving check" to determine if the client has experienced any significant cravings between session. This procedure is also a reminder for the client to remain vigilant for cravings.

15. One helpful way to cope with craving and urges to use substances is a meditation imagery technique known as *urge surfing* (Marlatt, 1985). Given that most clients believe that unless they satisfy their cravings (strong desire or appetite for drug effects) by giving into their urges (intent to use), the craving will continue to build until they feel "wiped out" by the increased intensity of their drug appetites. By giving in and using when the urge is at its peak, clients experience major negative reinforcement (relief from craving or unpleasant withdrawal symptoms), which strengthens their attachment to the addictive substance or activity. However, most urges are triggered by stimulus cues (cue reactivity) that precipitate a classically conditioned response (craving). If not reinforced by substance use, the urge will peak and then decline, usually in a fairly short period.

To help clients deal with the urge without giving in, clients are taught to visualize the urge as a rising ocean wave that they will learn to "surf" without getting "wiped out" by the craving and desire. First, the client is instructed to imagine experiencing a strong urge (perhaps facilitated by cue exposure) and to learn to "ride the urge" as a surfer would, by keeping one's balance as the wave passes beneath the surfboard.

Clients are instructed that the "surfboard" is associated with paying attention to the breath as it passes in (in breath) and out (out breath) as the wave passes through their body and mind. Awareness of the breath, as in other forms of meditation, provides a sense of balance and steadfastness as the craving wave crests and subsides on the other side. If the client becomes obsessed with the urge and distracted by thoughts of use, the attention is drawn back to the breath with a sense of nonjudgmental awareness and acceptance. Clients can be taught that the successful practice of this meditation technique will provide them with a skill that will help them manage many of these conditioned urge responses. Surf on!

Homework for Client

■ Use the Daily Craving Record to track your cravings over the next few months.

■ Complete the Substance Use Triggers Worksheet to help you identify triggers, the degree of threat each trigger represents, and strategies to help you cope with them.

Chapter 10 | *Managing Thoughts of Using Substances*

(Corresponds to chapter 9 of the workbook)

Materials Needed

- Managing Thoughts of Using Worksheet

Objectives

- To help the client become aware of how thoughts of using substances can contribute to relapse

- To help the client identify common thoughts and "apparently irrelevant decisions" that precede substance use

- To help the client learn strategies to manage and challenge thoughts of using alcohol, tobacco, or other drugs

Introduction

Clients have many different thoughts about using substances. Positive thoughts of using are commonly associated with many other recovery issues discussed in this manual, such as cravings, social pressures, family and interpersonal conflicts, and upsetting emotional states. Helping the client to become aware of and manage thoughts of using substances reduces the risk of relapse and raises the client's level of self-confidence.

Clients who experience a high-risk relapse situation and have positive thoughts of using are more vulnerable to taking a drink, smoking, or using other drugs. This is especially true if the client has little confidence in his or her ability to manage thoughts of using.

Some thoughts that can lead to relapse relate to:

- Belief that the substance problem has been solved (e.g., "I've got it beat now" or "I'll never use again")

- Limited use or testing personal control (e.g., "A few won't hurt")

- Having fun while sober (e.g., "I can't have fun if I don't use")

- Relaxation (e.g., "I need something to relax" or "I need something to take the edge off")

- Stress (e.g., "Life is difficult; I need to escape for a while")

- Socialization (e.g., "I can't fit in with others if they use and I don't")

- Motivation (e.g., "What's the point in staying sober; it doesn't matter")

Major Points and Issues for Discussion

The following are major points and issues for discussion:

1. The therapist discusses the relationship between thoughts, feelings, and behaviors. A client's beliefs and thoughts influence his or her feelings and actions. Cognitive distortions (or faulty ways of thinking) are associated with depression, anxiety, substance abuse, unhappiness, and numerous interpersonal problems (Beck, 1976; Beck et al., 1993; Burns, 1999; Newman et al., 2002) . Examples of various cognitive distortions are shown in Table 10.1.

2. The therapist discusses the relationship between thoughts of using and substance use behaviors. Thoughts of using can build up gradually over time or be experienced quickly and intensely.

3. The therapist discusses the concept of "apparently irrelevant decisions" (Marlatt, 1985). These are seemingly unimportant decisions that lead clients to rationalize behaviors that could contribute to a relapse set-up. For example, a client who recently quit drinking but keeps alcohol in her house "in case guests drop by" has made a decision that could have a major impact on relapse. A client who quits using cocaine but decides to attend a party "to see old friends"

Table 10.1 Examples of Cognitive Distortions

Type of error	Example
Personalizing	Thinking all situations and events revolve around oneself: "Everyone was looking at me and wondering why I was there."
Magnifying	Blowing negative events out of proportion: "This is the worst thing that could happen to me."
Minimizing	Glossing over positive factors; overlooking the fact that nothing really bad happened.
Either/or thinking	Not taking into account the full continuum: "Either I'm a loser or a winner."
Taking events out of context	After a successful interview, focusing on one or two tough questions: "I blew the interview."
Jumping to conclusions	Reaching conclusions without all the facts of a situation: "I have a swollen gland. This must be cancer."
Overgeneralizing	Taking one or two experiences and reaching major conclusions that apply to all situations: "I always fail. I fail at everything I ever try."
Self-blame	Blaming the total self rather then specific behaviors that can be changed: "I'm no good."
Magical thinking	"Everything is bad because of my bad past deeds."
Mind reading	"Everyone there thought I was fat and ugly."
Comparing	Comparing oneself with someone else and ignoring all the basic differences: "Regina's figure is better than mine."
Catastrophizing	Putting the worst possible construction on events: "I know something terrible happened."

Adapted from Burns (1999).

puts his recovery in jeopardy by being in social situations in which he is likely to feel direct or indirect pressure to use cocaine.

4. The client needs to be aware of thoughts of using and the context in which they occur. For example, thoughts of using substances may increase following interpersonal conflicts, upsetting emotions, disappointments, or even positive experiences.

5. When the client discusses strong cravings for substances, close calls, or actual lapses or relapses, the therapist inquires about what thoughts he or she experienced prior to and during the particular situation. This will help raise awareness of the role of cognition in emotional reactions and behaviors.

Managing Thoughts of Using Worksheet

Instructions: Review the list of common thoughts associated with relapse. Add some personal thoughts to the list. Then, list counterstatements and strategies you can use to change these thoughts in order to control them and prevent them from leading to substance use.

	Thoughts	Counterstatements
1.	I'll never use again. I've got my problem under control.	Never is a long time; even though I'm not drinking, I still have to remain vigilant.
2.	A few cigarettes (drinks, lines of cocaine, etc.) won't hurt.	True, a few won't hurt, but my drinking pattern is to overdo it. I never stop at a few, so a few will hurt me. I don't like to, but total sobriety is necessary for me.
3.	I can't have fun or excitement if I don't use.	Says who? I have some things that I enjoy, that are fun. The truth is, I don't need to drink to have fun. I have to take responsibility and make sure I build some fun into my daily life.
4.	I need something to take the edge off and help me relax.	There are other ways of relaxing. I can take a walk, exercise, listen to music, or read.
5.	Life is difficult. I need to escape for awhile.	Sure, life is hard sometimes, but not just for me, for a lot of others, too. I can get away from stress for a while without drinking.
6.	I can't fit in with others if they use and I don't.	This is only true for problem drinkers. I know people who drink socially, who don't overdo it. They don't care if I drink or not. I don't need to fit in with the heavy drinkers because it's too much pressure.
7.	What's the point in staying sober? It really doesn't matter.	Who said staying sober was easy? It does matter a lot if I stay sober. My health will be better, I can be a better mother to my daughter. And, I can keep my life on track only if I'm sober.

Figure 10.1

Example of a completed Managing Thoughts of Using Worksheet.

8. *I'm going to test myself to see if I can have just one.*	A better way to testing myself is to see if I can have none. If I have one, I will only want more.
9. *How can I go out with Leroy if I don't drink?*	Leroy doesn't drink too much. I can tell him about my drinking problem. I can enjoy his company without drinking.
10. *I'll never get out of debt, I might as well get drunk.*	Things were much worse when I was drinking. At least now, I can pay my bills and care for my daughter even if things are tight. There's no excuse for getting drunk now.
11. *I could drink and no one would ever know.*	I would know and wouldn't be fooling anyone but myself. I can choose not to drink. I will choose not to drink.

Figure 10.1 *continued*

6. Because thoughts of using substances are common, especially during the early weeks and months of recovery, it is important to have strategies to challenge these thoughts. Otherwise, the risk of relapse increases.

7. The client completes the Managing Thoughts of Using Worksheet (Figure 10.1). This worksheet provides common examples of substance-related thoughts and asks the client to identify additional thoughts. The client then devises counterstatements to help manage thoughts of using. This exercise helps the client practice changing common thoughts of using. In the long run, the client needs to be able to challenge other specific thought of using when they occur.

8. To help the client challenge and dispute thoughts of using, the therapist reviews the strategies discussed in the previous chapter on coping with cravings, such as (a) reviewing the benefits of not drinking, smoking, or ingesting drugs; (b) thinking about the long-term, positive effects of remaining abstinent versus the short-term, perceived benefits of using; (c) reviewing the adverse effects

of previous substance use as a reminder of the potential negative consequences of giving in to thoughts of using; (d) distracting oneself by thinking about something pleasant, fun, or enjoyable such as a past experience, upcoming event, or vacation; and (e) sharing thoughts with others, especially those in recovery who can offer acceptance, support, and advice.

9. The therapist teaches the client to negotiate with the "inner self" by buying time and putting off the decision to use for several hours or longer. For example, the client may say, "I'll wait until tomorrow to use." Simply buying oneself time is often sufficient to deal with thoughts of using substances.

Homework for Client

■ Complete the Managing Thoughts of Using Worksheet to help you practice new ways of thinking.

Chapter 11 | *Managing Emotions*

(Corresponds to chapter 10 of the workbook)

Materials Needed

■ Emotions Worksheet

Objectives

■ To identify the role of negative or positive emotions in recovery and relapse

■ To help the client identify high-risk emotional issues (specific emotions or deficits in coping skills) to address in recovery

■ To help the client learn appropriate strategies for managing emotions

Introduction

Ineffective responses to negative emotional states are the most common relapse precipitants, and they pose a challenge for the client in recovery (Daley & Marlatt, 2005; Marlatt & Donovan, 2005). Negative emotional states can be exacerbated by physical withdrawal as well as by life problems, stresses, and interpersonal difficulties. In addition to having an impact on relapse, negative affect such as anger, depression, anxiety, boredom, loneliness, guilt, or shame causes unhappiness and distress and contributes to interpersonal difficulties. In some instances negative affect is a symptom of a psychiatric disorder.

Clients may use substances to cover up these emotions or to help cope with them. However, the effects of alcohol or other drugs exaggerate emotions and impair judgment. This in turn leads to the client's inappropriately acting on emotions. For example, mild frustration or anger can be expressed as intense hatred, or normal attraction can be expressed as unremitting love.

Clients may have difficulty recognizing their emotions or blame others for what they feel. Following is a brief listing of difficulties related to upsetting emotions experienced by clients with alcohol or drug problems:

- *Anger.* Expressing it too freely or verbally or in physically harmful ways; letting it build and avoiding direct expression of it when appropriate; letting it control behavior; failure to acknowledge anger toward others; inability to let go of angry feelings toward others; excessive anger at self for having a substance use disorder

- *Anxiety.* Fear or worry about one's ability to stick to recovery, or about specific problems in life; fear that leads to avoidant behaviors and adversely affects the client's ability to function or attend recovery group meetings; persistent and disabling anxiety or fear that does not improve with sobriety or worsens with abstinence and that is symptomatic of a psychiatric disorder

- *Boredom.* Difficulty having fun without planning to use or actually using substances; inability to enjoy experiences in which substances are not available; trouble adjusting to the routine of sobriety; discovering serious boredom with a job or primary relationship upon getting sober

- *Depression.* Feeling sad due to losses caused by the substance use problem; feeling sad and hopeless about serious problems in career, health, relationships, or some other major aspect of life; having a persistent mood disorder that does not appear to improve or worsens with continued sobriety

- *Emptiness.* Feeling a void in which little pleasure, satisfaction, or meaning in life is experienced; feeling persistent emptiness that doesn't abate with longer-term sobriety and may be part of a mood or personality disorder; wondering, "Is this all there is?" after a period of sobriety of several months or longer

- *Guilt and shame.* Feeling bad about one's actions or inactions related to substance use; feeling bad, defective, or like a failure for having a substance use problem

- *Loneliness.* Feeling lonely because the substance use disorder contributed to failed relationships; inability to establish and maintain a close, interpersonal relationship

When clients stop using substances, they often need to learn to manage emotions in new ways. Some clients have to learn to recognize their feelings and give themselves permission to experience them because they are so out of touch with their emotions. Others need to learn self-control and how to tolerate emotional distress without acting in self-destructive or violent ways. Many clients need help in learning to cope with emotions in responsible, productive ways that lead to continued sobriety, better mental health, improved interpersonal relationships, and improved health (Daley & Douaihy, 2005).

Major Points and Issues for Discussion

The following are major points and issues for discussion:

1. The therapist discusses how negative emotional states contribute to relapse, dissatisfaction in life, health problems, or problematic relationships. There is also the possibility that positive emotional states (e.g., excitement, celebration, and strong sexual passions) may serve as triggers, especially in an interpersonal context. Some clients use substances to dampen or control any strong affect, positive or negative. It is important to be able to manage emotions in recovery. Some clients find this difficult when they first stop using substances.

2. The client completes the Emotions Worksheet (Figure 11.1) to rate the degree of difficulty dealing with anxiety and worry, anger, boredom, depression, emptiness, guilt, shame, and loneliness without relying on substances. This worksheet also helps the client begin to formulate strategies for managing emotions.

3. The therapist assesses the client's general style of dealing with negative affect. Are upsetting emotions denied, avoided, suppressed, acted out in ways harmful to others, or acted out in ways harmful to the client? Which emotional states are likely to influence the client to use alcohol, tobacco, or other drugs? Which cause the most difficulty in other areas of life or lead to significant personal distress? To become more aware of his or her positive and problematic coping styles, the client can use a journal to record and rate the intensity of emotions, the context in which they occur, and coping strategies used.

4. The therapist helps the client deal with specific problematic emotions. This requires the client to be able to recognize and accept emotional states rather than rationalizing or suppressing them. This also requires the client to be able to identify problems associated with emotion and his or her normal style of coping. For example, suppressing anger and expressing it through passive-aggressive behaviors often leads to interpersonal conflict and dissatisfaction. If a husband is angry at his wife and unable to express it directly, he may express it indirectly. He may "forget" important dates such as his wife's birthday or their anniversary, which can lead to ill feelings and marital strife.

5. The therapist helps the client figure out what may be contributing to the occurrence of a particular emotional state so that problems can be solved. For example, if a client is depressed due to severe interpersonal conflict associated with an abusive relationship, the relationship may have to be changed so the client can improve the depressed mood. If a client is lonely and disconnected from other people because he or she becomes too dependent in relationships and drives others away with his or her insatiable needs, this pattern will need to be changed so the client can develop appropriate relationships that are mutually beneficial.

6. The therapist helps the client examine and change faulty beliefs and thoughts that may contribute to a specific emotional conflict. For example, thoughts associated with anger, such as, "It's bad to get angry" and "If I get angry, I'll lose it and hurt someone" can be changed to "It's normal to get angry; everyone feels this at times"

Emotions Worksheet

Instructions: For each emotion below, rate the degree of difficulty you have dealing with these feelings without using alcohol or drugs. Then, choose the two emotions that present the most difficulty in your recovery and identify strategies for coping with them.

0 ———————— 1 ———————— 2 ———————— 3 ———————— 4 ———————— 5

None   Low   Moderate   Severe

Emotion	Degree of difficulty coping with emotion (0–5)
1. Anxiety and worry	2
2. Anger	5
3. Boredom	5
4. Depression	3
5. Feeling empty—like nothing matters	3
6. Guilt	4
7. Shame	3
8. Loneliness	3

Feeling or emotion	Coping strategies
Boredom	Plan weekends in advance to limit free time on my hands; build in pleasurable activities every single week; accept some boredom as normal and inevitable; tell myself this is a chance to try something new.
Anger	Don't let little things get me so worked up; think things through when I'm angry before I act on them; keep my voice normal when talking to my wife about my anger; remind myself that I can stay in control when angry.

Figure 11.1

Example of a completed Emotions Worksheet.

or "I can get angry without losing control and getting violent." Thoughts associated with boredom, such as, "I always have to be doing something," "I won't be able to entertain myself," and "Life can't be any fun without substances" can be changed to "I don't need action all the time; it's OK to slow down," "I'm fully capable of finding ways to entertain and enjoy myself," "I can have fun without alcohol or other drugs," or "What evidence is there that a person like me can't have fun without using?" Thoughts associated with depression, such as, "It would be terrible if others didn't accept or like me," "I can't make mistakes," and "The worst possible thing is going to happen" can be changed to "There's no way everyone is going to accept or like me; it's just part of life," "Mistakes are normal, so why make a big deal out of any mistakes that I make?" and "What evidence do I have that the worst thing is always going to happen?"

7. The therapist encourages the client to express emotions directly to others when appropriate or share them with a trusted friend. Learning to disclose feelings is difficult for many clients. Some will need help in learning to talk with others about their feelings. In some instances, clients need to learn assertiveness so that they can stand up for themselves and deal with anger, frustration, disappointment, and conflict with another person.

8. The client should increase structure in daily life. Too much free time, particularly when coupled with a lack of goals, is a high-risk situation for many substance users. Structure can reduce anxiety, boredom, and depression, especially when pleasant activities are included.

9. The therapist encourages the client to regularly participate in physical, social, and creative activities. These activities can help reduce stress and release tension and other feelings.

10. The therapist encourages the client to read about emotional issues by providing specific recommendations of books or recovery guides. Many informative, inspirational, and hopeful materials are available on virtually any area of emotional difficulty.

11. The client can also use "inner-directed" activities such as meditation or prayer. Such activities can reduce negative feelings, increase energy, and improve the client's outlook on life.

12. The therapist should consider a medication evaluation for serious negative emotional states (e.g., depression, anxiety) that persist even if the client uses some of the previously discussed strategies. Many clients with substance use problems experience a mood or anxiety disorder at some point in their lives. In some instances, the disorder is severe enough to cause personal distress and difficulty functioning. In addition to therapy, non-addictive medications can be quite helpful in treating such disorders. Self-help groups for psychiatric disorders can also help the client gain social support and learn additional strategies for coping with feelings.

13. Although many clients struggle with negative affect, the therapist should also discuss positive emotional states. For example, helping clients increase their ability to appropriately share positive feelings (e.g., love) often makes them feel better and improves their interpersonal relationships. Discussion should not focus solely on negative affect.

Homework for Client

- Complete the Emotions Worksheet to identify and rate the emotional states you need to address in your recovery.

- Develop your own recovery coping strategies.

Chapter 12 | *Refusing Offers to Use Substances*

(Corresponds to chapter 11 of the workbook)

Materials Needed

- Social Pressures Worksheet

Objectives

- To help the client identify direct and indirect social pressures (people, places, events, social and work situations) to use alcohol, tobacco, or other drugs

- To identify feelings experienced during social pressure situations (e.g., anger, anxiety, excitement)

- To identify thoughts experienced during social pressure situations (e.g., wanting to fit in, wanting to be normal)

- To identify strategies to avoid high-risk people, places, situations, and events and to cope with social pressures that cannot be avoided

Introduction

One of the most common challenges for any client giving up alcohol, tobacco, or other drugs is resisting social pressures to use substances (Daley, 2004a; Marlatt & Donovan, 2005). Social pressures are the second most common relapse precipitants. Clients who are not prepared to resist pressures to use are more vulnerable to relapse.

Direct social pressures include situations in which others offer the client substances. Pressure may vary from mild to extreme, in which another person tries very hard to influence the client to use. The client may feel anxious, awkward, and tempted to use. In some social interactions, the possibility of a sexual encounter may be intertwined with alcohol or other drug use, adding to the pressure felt to use substances.

The client is also likely to experience indirect social pressure during situations in which alcohol, tobacco, or other drugs are being used but no one is directly pressuring the client to use substances. The desire to use can be very high in such situations. For example, a person who gives up alcohol and attends a work-related social function where others are drinking can feel tempted. A person who has given up smoking can be at a party or in a restaurant where others are smoking and feel pressure to smoke, from smelling smoke or seeing others smoke.

Because avoiding all people who use substances and events and situations in which others may be using substances is not possible, the client needs to prepare to resist any social pressure he or she encounters. Preparing ahead of time can make the client feel more comfortable and confident when handling various direct and indirect social pressures to use substances.

Major Points and Issues for Discussion

The following are major points and issues for discussion:

1. The therapist discusses how social pressures, both direct and indirect, affect relapse, and emphasizes the importance of identifying social pressures and having strategies to avoid or resist them.

2. The client completes the Social Pressures Worksheet (Figure 12.1) to identify specific people who might pressure the client and places, events, and situations in which social pressures are likely to be experienced. The therapist can use the client's difficulty rating for each social pressure to prioritize those that represent the greatest or most immediate relapse risk.

3. The therapist helps the client identify which pressures represent the greatest challenge to recovery, and ascertains the client's level of confidence in successfully resisting these pressures to use. For

Social Pressures Worksheet

Instructions: List specific direct or indirect social pressures to use alcohol, tobacco, or other drugs that you expect to face. For each social pressure you list, use the scale below to rate the degree of difficulty you believe you will have coping successfully with that pressure. Finally, list coping strategies you can use to cope with these social pressures.

```
0 —————— 1 —————— 2 —————— 3 —————— 4 —————— 5
```

No Threat   Moderate Threat   Severe Threat

Social pressures	Degree of difficulty (0–5)	Coping strategies
Mark (brother)	4	Don't go to bars or clubs. Tell Mark, Sam, and
Sam (brother-in-law)	5	Jack I'm not drinking anymore and ask them
Jack (drinking buddy)	4	not to pressure me to have a few. Leave after
		softball games instead of staying around and
		drinking. Leave Mark's garage if the guys
		drink. Stop monthly poker games until I feel
		like I can handle them.
Ballpark	3	Plan non-drinking activities for picnics. Tell
Brother's garage	4	myself I can have a good time without
Red's Bar & Grill	5	drinking.
Family picnics	4	Develop new hobbies that don't involve
Get-togethers at Mike's house	4	drinking. Attend social events at local
Annual work Christmas party	5	recovery club.
Monthly poker games	4	

Figure 12.1

Example of a completed Social Pressures Worksheet.

Instructions: List specific direct or indirect social pressures to use alcohol, tobacco, or other drugs that you expect to face. For each social pressure you list, use the scale below to rate the degree of difficulty you believe you will have coping successfully with that pressure. Finally, list coping strategies you can use to cope with these social pressures.

0 ——————— 1 ——————— 2 ——————— 3 ——————— 4 ——————— 5

No Threat   Moderate Threat   Severe Threat

Social pressures	Degree of difficulty (0–5)	Coping strategies
Husband	4	Ask husband not to smoke in front of me
Smokers at work	5	at home. Request smokers to smoke
Friends who smoke	4	outside when visiting my house.
Home	4	Spend more time with non-smoking friends.
Any friend's home	4	Change habits at work to avoid smoking
Restaurants	3	at coffee breaks or after lunch. Request
		non-smoking section at restaurants and
		ask husband for his support.
Dinner out	3	Have gum or mints with me when at
Break time at work	3/4	someone else's home who smokes.
Socializing with friends	4	
who smoke	5	
Morning coffee or dinner		
at home with husband		

Figure 12.1 *continued*

example, a client who worries she will not fit in with peers who drink, or who thinks she can't have any fun if others drink, is likely to experience strong pressures to use alcohol. A client who anticipates, prepares for, and feels confident that she has the skills to cope with social pressures has a greater chance of successfully coping with these pressures.

4. The therapist and client explore the nuances of social pressure situations to see if there is more going on than meets the eye. For example, it isn't uncommon for some clients to put their recovery at risk for the opportunity to experience a sexual encounter. Some clients minimize or deny the risks associated with such interpersonal interactions. Also, some clients experience relapse set-ups by putting themselves in situations in which they are likely to be pressured to use substances. For example, a client with an alcohol problem who is new to recovery and who goes to the local club to socialize with drinking buddies with the intention of drinking "only soda" raises his vulnerability to drinking. The same hold true for the ex-smoker who joins colleagues at work during their smoking break.

5. Some clients will be involved in a social network composed mainly of active substance abusers, involved in a primary relationship (spouse, partner, roommate) with a substance abuser, or work in a situation where substances are used or abused. The client will need to carefully evaluate these situations to determine how to cope with them. These situations represent a major threat to many clients and often require significant changes.

6. The therapist helps the client become aware of feelings generated by social pressures. Feelings may range from excitement and positive anticipation to anxiety or dread. In early recovery, the client is likely to feel ambivalent: on the one hand, he or she would like to give in to pressures to use; on the other hand, he or she would like to remain sober.

7. The therapist helps the client become aware of thoughts generated by social pressures, such as, "I can't fit in unless I use" or "What's the big deal about a few drinks or cigarettes?" Then, the therapist can help the client change his or her specific thoughts. Thoughts

and feelings generated by social pressures determine what a client does to cope.

8. The therapist discusses the importance of avoiding certain high-risk people, places, events, and situations. For example, bars, parties in which alcohol is used excessively or drugs are available, and socializing with active substance abusers or addicts are common high-risk situations that can usually be avoided.

9. Many clients benefit from behavioral rehearsals or role-plays in which they practice specific ways of assertively refusing offers to use substances. The therapist can help the client use different words, tones of voice, and body language to feel confident to resist pressures to use.

10. Clients can offset the potential impact of social influences on relapse by eliciting support from a recovery treatment group, self-help group, or friend or family member (see Chapter 14 for a review of recovery support systems).

Homework for Client

▤ Complete the Social Pressures Worksheet.

Chapter 13 | *Dealing With Family and Interpersonal Problems*

(Corresponds to chapter 12 of the workbook)

Materials Needed

- Family Effects Worksheet
- Relationships Worksheet
- Interpersonal Style Worksheet

Objectives

- To identify effects of the substance use disorder on family and interpersonal relationships
- To help the client identify strategies to cope with family and interpersonal problems caused by the substance use
- To help the client improve interpersonal effectiveness

Introduction

Family and interpersonal problems are common in recovery for individuals with any substance use disorder, including those with co-occurring psychiatric disorders (Daley & Sinberg-Spear, 2003). Interpersonal conflict is the third most common relapse risk factor among alcoholics, smokers, and heroin addicts (Marlatt & Donovan, 2005).

Addressing family and interpersonal issues in treatment offers many potential advantages for clients, who can both address significant issues and increase specific interpersonal skills. These advantages include:

- Helps reverse some of the damage to family or social relationships caused by the substance use disorder

- Helps increase the likelihood that the family members or significant others will get involved in treatment and/or mutual support groups like Al-Anon or Nar-Anon to address their needs

- Increases the likelihood that the client will get support from others

- Helps the client acquire skills to resist social pressures to use substances

- Helps the client develop social support networks

- Helps the client assess and improve family and social relationships

- Helps the client assess and improve communication skills

- Improves the client's ability to address and resolve specific interpersonal problems

- Increases the client's satisfaction with relationships

Many of the NIAAA, NIDA, CSAT, and other treatment manuals include varying degrees of focus on these interpersonal and family issues in recovery from alcohol or drug use disorders (e.g., CSAT, 2004b; Monti et al., 2002; NIAAA, 1995a, 1995b, 1995c; NIDA, 1998a, 1998b, 1999a, 2003; O'Farrell & Fals-Stewart, 1999). For example, the *Coping Skills Training* model developed by Monti and colleagues (2002) for alcohol dependence has two main areas of focus in teaching clients cognitive and behavioral skills to aid recovery: interpersonal skills and intrapersonal skills. Interpersonal skills in this model include communication skills, drink refusal skills, resolving interpersonal problems, and developing social support networks.

Family Effects Worksheet

Instructions: List your family members. Then, describe ways in which the behaviors related to your substance use problem have affected each family member.

Family member	Behaviors/consequences of my substance use
Parents	Borrowed money and never paid it back; stole checks and forged them; never took an interest in parents; used them to bail me out of trouble; upset and worried them, and caused them to be distrustful toward me.
Wife	Lied to her; ignored her; used family income to buy drugs; sold some of her jewelry; she became so distressed and hurt, she left me.
Son	Missed many important events when he was small; didn't spend enough time with him; hard on him when my wife and I separated because of my drug problem.
Brother	Sometimes, I didn't show up for work when I was supposed to help him; created excuses and lies to cover my tracks; disappointed him; he knew I was having drug problems and worried about me.

Figure 13.1

Example of a completed Family Effects Worksheet.

Major Points and Issues for Discussion

The following are major points and issues for discussion:

1. The therapist discusses how substance use problems affect the family. The client completes the Family Effects Worksheet (Figure 13.1). This worksheet has the client identify specific family members adversely affected by the client's substance use. The client also provides examples of problem behaviors and their impact on the family.

2. When reviewing this worksheet with the client, the therapist asks for more details when appropriate. For example, if a client reported missing important events in the life of his child, the therapist would ask for specific examples, such as birthdays or graduations. How does the client feel about the relationship being discussed and about having hurt the family member? Clients may feel guilty and ashamed, and some may deny or minimize the adverse effects of their substance use on their family, especially on their children. The therapist can help the client understand the family's experience by inquiring about what it was like for a specific family member to be exposed to the client's substance use and related behaviors.

3. If the client is involved in a 12-step program such as AA or NA, the therapist can discuss the effects on the family in the context of steps 8 and 9 (the "making amends" steps).

4. The therapist discusses how the client's substance use affected other interpersonal relationships. The client completes the Relationships Worksheet (Figure 13.2). This worksheet helps the client identify specific interpersonal problems and formulate strategies for improving them.

5. The therapist helps the client prioritize interpersonal problems so he or she can deal first with the greatest threats to recovery. Common relationship problems that interfere with recovery include involvement with family members, a partner, or friends who are active substance abusers; lack of healthy or supportive relationships; or involvement in relationships characterized by chronic chaos or excessive criticism.

6. When exploring specific interpersonal relationship problems, the therapist helps the client view the reciprocal nature of relationships and his or her role in these problems. Clients often blame relationship problems on the other person and deny or minimize responsibility for their own roles.

7. The therapist asks the client what steps can be taken to begin dealing with the adverse impact that his or her substance use problem has had on family members. Both general strategies (e.g., inviting family members to attend counseling sessions or self-help meet-

Relationships Worksheet

Instructions: Describe the problematic relationships in your life. Write about what you can do to improve these relationships.

Problem	Ways to improve problem
I get too easily angry at my son helping him with homework.	Keep in mind he's only in fourth grade and remind myself to be more patient; take a break if I feel too upset with him until I cool off; give him positive feedback when his work is neat and done correctly; and ask my husband to help our son during times in which I feel too stressed out.
Tension between me and my older sister.	Invite her over for lunch; bring up my concerns and engage her in discussion to figure out how we can get our relationship back on track.
Don't get out alone with husband enough.	Stop making excuses that we are too busy and regularly plan fun activities; let him know I want more alone time with him, that it's important to me; plan a surprise date with him.

Figure 13.2

Example of a completed Relationships Worksheet.

ings, providing educational materials to the family) and specific strategies (e.g., concrete ways of improving a specific relationship with a child or spouse) can be discussed.

8. The client is encouraged to initiate open discussions with family members regarding the substance use problem and change plan. If the client is too worried or feels unable to do this, the therapist can ask the client to bring the family to sessions to discuss these issues. The client needs to understand that family members may have some reactions and feelings that may be difficult to hear.

9. The therapist discusses the potential risk and benefits of inviting the client's family to become involved in the recovery process. Some family members will be helpful and supportive, but others

may be angry, hostile, and resistant to supporting the recovering member in this way.

10. The therapist can invite the family to individual or group sessions to help them learn about substance use problems and the recovery process, and to provide them with an opportunity to talk about their experiences, questions, and concerns. This can be an effective strategy to overcome the client's resistance related to involving the family. Also, a discussion with the family enables the clinician to intervene in such a way to help the family overcome resistance to getting involved in treatment.

11. The therapist can encourage the client to invite family members to family support groups such as Al-Anon, Nar-Anon, Alateen, or Adult Children of Alcoholics (ACOA). The therapist can also directly invite the family to attend such meetings.

12. The therapist determines if there are any serious problems in the family that might require further evaluation or treatment. The therapist then facilitates any evaluations needed. For example, if a client reports that a teenage daughter is very depressed and suicidal and is not receiving any type of mental health care, the therapist helps the client arrange for an evaluation of the daughter.

13. Clients who are farther along in recovery, with substantial sober time, can benefit from exploring and changing their interpersonal behaviors. Such clients should complete the Interpersonal Style Worksheet (Figure 13.3). This worksheet will help identify the client's interpersonal strengths as well as aspects of interpersonal style that play a role in relationship problems.

14. After problems related to interpersonal style have been identified, the therapist can help the client examine and change interpersonal deficits. For example, if a client identified shyness or lack of assertiveness as an interpersonal problem, the client and therapist would explore specific ways in which these problems could be addressed. Behavioral rehearsals are often effective in helping clients begin to develop more effective communication or assertiveness skills. Cognitive interventions are often effective in getting clients to change their beliefs about how they should communicate and behave in their relationships.

Interpersonal Style Worksheet

Instructions: Following is a list of statements about interpersonal style. In the second column, circle the number that corresponds to the extent to which each statement describes you. Then complete the two items below the list of statements.

	Doesn't describe me		Somewhat describes me		Definitely describes me
1. I say what I think or feel to others and don't hold anything back.	o 1	2	3	4	(5)
2. I worry about hurting others and hold on to my feelings.	(0) 1	2	3	4	5
3. I lash out at others when I'm upset or mad at them.	o 1	2	3	(4)	5
4. I regularly share positive feelings with others.	o 1	2	3	(4)	5
5. I often criticize others a lot and express negative feelings.	o 1	2	3	4	(5)
6. I have trouble talking to strangers.	o 1	(2)	3	4	5
7. I consider myself to be shy and have trouble opening up to others.	o (1)	2	3	4	5
8. I relate easily to others and like meeting new people.	o 1	(2)	3	4	5
9. I let other people close to me know what's important to me.	o 1	2	3	(4)	5
10. I don't like to argue with others and avoid arguments when I can.	o 1	(2)	3	4	5
11. I let people take advantage of me too easily.	(0) 1	2	3	4	5
12. I consider myself to be an aggressive person.	o 1	2	3	4	(5)
13. I consider myself to be an assertive person.	o 1	2	3	4	(5)
14. I consider myself to be a pushover and a passive person.	(0) 1	2	3	4	5
15. I avoid situations where I have to talk in front of other people.	o 1	(2)	3	4	5
16. I use alcohol, tobacco, or other drugs to help me socialize with others.	o 1	(2)	3	4	5

Identify one aspect of your interpersonal style that you want to change.

I often criticize others and express negative feelings.

List several steps you can take to help you change this behavior.

I'm most critical of my wife and kids, so I'll start by not yelling at them in a nasty voice; I'll think about why I'm feeling negative toward them and be more realistic about what I expect; I'll also consciously make efforts to say something positive to my wife and kids every day, so that I'm not always focused on the negative.

Figure 13.3
Example of a completed Interpersonal Style Worksheet.

- Complete the Relationships Worksheet.

- Complete the Interpersonal Style Worksheet.

- Complete the Family Effects Worksheet.

Chapter 14 | *Building a Recovery Support System*

(Corresponds to chapter 13 of the workbook)

Materials Needed

▦ Recovery Network Worksheet

Objectives

▦ To review the client's current social support system to identify the nature of current relationships

▦ To identify the benefits of having a recovery support system

▦ To identify specific individuals and organizations that the client can include in his or her support network

▦ To help the client become aware of and overcome any specific barriers to asking for help and support

Introduction

A positive social support system is associated with better outcome for clients who are overcoming alcohol or drug problems (Daley & Marlatt, 2005). Healthy and supportive relationships with family, friends, and other recovering individuals offer many potential benefits. The pressure to use substances decreases, the tendency to isolate oneself lessens, there are opportunities to reach out for help and support in times of stress, and there are opportunities to share mutual interest or experiences. Very importantly, others in recovery can offer the client strength, hope, and advice on ways to handle specific challenges of recovery, such as how to manage cravings; manage people, places, events, and things; deal with negative thinking about recovery; or make lifestyle changes necessary for long-term recovery.

In addition to specific people, organizations can be a major part of a client's recovery support system. Virtually any organization can be important to a given client. Possibilities include church, community, athletic, or recovery-oriented organizations, or those based on the specific needs and interests of the client. Chapter 15 focuses on self-help programs and recovery clubs, which play a crucial role in the recovery of many clients with substance use disorders.

There are, however, numerous barriers to asking for help and support. Clients whose social networks consist mainly of others who abuse or are dependent on alcohol or other drugs may be reluctant to cut their ties with these people, especially if they have long-term relationships. Some clients are so independent and self-reliant that they prefer to work things out on their own and don't like asking others for help or support, no matter how small the request may be. Others are shy or socially anxious, lack self-confidence, or have poor social skills, making it difficult for them to know how to ask for help or support. In some instances, social anxiety and avoidant behavior are part of a more serious problem, such as social phobia. These clients may not know whom to approach or even what to say. Yet others operate with the belief that they are not worthy of help from others or they will be rejected if they ask for it. Such beliefs create a barrier to building a recovery support system.

Major Points and Issues for Discussion

The following are major points and issues for discussion:

1. The therapist reviews the client's current social network to get a perspective on his or her relationships. Do any significant relationships exist with others who actively abuse alcohol or other drugs? If so, how much of a threat do these relationships pose to the client's recovery? The therapist should find out whom the client trusts and whom the client feels can provide help and support in his or her attempts to change.

2. The therapist discusses the relationship between having a recovery support system and positive outcome in recovery. Clients who have support from family and friends generally do better in recovery than those who lack social support or who have negative social networks.

3. It is important to have a range of people—family members, friends, and others in recovery—in a recovery support system. The client should be with people who can offer support, not those who will be negative, critical, or unsupportive of his or her efforts to change.

4. The therapist discusses the role that organizations (e.g., church, community) can play in the client's ongoing recovery. Find out organizations in which the client would like to be involved, and discuss ways to go about this.

5. The client completes the Recovery Network Worksheet (Figure 14.1). This worksheet will help the client identify specific people and organizations and the potential benefits of each in ongoing recovery. Some clients may be unable to identify relationships with people who do not have a substance use problem. If a client is unable to identify any specific person or organization that can support his or her recovery, the therapist and client need to explore the reasons for this. If necessary, the therapist can give specific suggestions on where the client may begin to establish some supportive relationships (e.g., at self-help meetings).

6. The therapist points out that people in recovery sometimes have difficulty asking others for help and support. Some of the barriers to asking for help are (a) pride and excessive self-reliance, (b) shyness and social anxiety, (c) lack of social skills in communicating and interacting with others, (d) lack of self-confidence, and (e) negative beliefs about self (e.g., "I don't deserve for anyone to help me") or others (e.g., "No one really cares about me" or "You can't depend on anyone else").

7. If the client identifies these or other major barriers to reaching out to others, the therapist discusses the reasons as well as strategies to overcome these barriers. Sometimes, changing beliefs will lead to a

Recovery Network Worksheet

Instructions: Identify people and organizations that you believe can be a vital part of your recovery network. Then list the potential benefits of having these individuals and organizations as part of your recovery.

People/organizations	Potential benefits
Nurses recovery group	Chance to be with other nurses in recovery to talk about special problems we face; might feel more comfortable and able to talk about my drug problem; others have told me this group has been real helpful; can help me save my career in nursing.
NA meetings	Learn additional ways to stay drug free; place to talk about things bothering me; ways to meet drug-free people; can participate in NA-sponsored social events.
Linda (NA sponsor)	Can share personal things hard to bring up in groups; can share my small victories as well as struggles in recovery; she can help me with the 12-step program.
Parents	They've always been behind me and will do everything to support my recovery; regular visits will keep me close with them.
Sim and Terri	They've both been clean for a long time and can help me understand what to expect and how to stay clean; we can share support; and it will be safe to do social activities with them.

Figure 14.1

Example of a completed Recovery Network Worksheet.

change in the client's behavior. In other instances, the client may need help in developing appropriate social skills, such as initiating conversations, disclosing personal information about himself or herself, and making specific requests to others. Many clients know what they should do to elicit support but feel awkward, uncomfortable, or unworthy; others fail to ask for support because they simply do not know how.

8. A significant minority of clients with substance use disorders have high levels of social anxiety that lead them to avoid people, self-help programs, groups, or participation in community activities. Client often don't spontaneously share this information; on the surface, they may appear resistant to actively developing a recovery support system. Self-administered questionnaires on anxiety, phobias, depression, or other problems can be used during the assessment process to identify clients who have significant levels of anxiety, avoidant behavior, or other problems that adversely impact their ability to use social support.

9. The therapist can encourage the client to participate in pleasant activities involving other people on a regular basis. Having fun and participating in social interactions makes the process of recovery more enjoyable and rewarding and helps the client stay connected to others.

Homework for Client

▪ Complete the Recovery Network Worksheet.

Chapter 15 | *Self-Help Programs and Recovery Clubs*

(Corresponds to chapter 14 of the workbook)

Materials Needed

- Self-Help Program Worksheet

Objectives

- To provide the client with information about self-help programs and recovery clubs

- To help the client identify drawbacks and benefits of attending self-help programs and recovery clubs

- To help the client identify specific self-help programs that can enhance his or her recovery

Introduction

Mutual support programs are effective in helping clients in their ongoing recovery from substance use problems (Emrick & Tonigan, 2004; Hazelden Foundation, 2004). The most common programs are Alcoholics Anonymous (AA) and Narcotics Anonymous (NA). Some areas have other 12-step programs for specific types of drug abuse or dependence such as Cocaine Anonymous or Marijuana Anonymous.

There are also 12-step programs for clients who are trying to quit tobacco use, Smokers Anonymous and Nicotine Anonymous, but these are not available in many communities. A 12-step program called Dual Recovery Anonymous (DRA) is available for clients who have both a substance use disorder and a psychiatric disorder. Unfortunately, DRA meetings are not as numerous as AA or NA meetings, and many areas have none at all.

Other self-help programs include Women for Sobriety (WFS), Men for Sobriety (MFS), Rational Recovery (RR), and Self-Management and Recovery Training (SMART). These programs are also less available than AA or NA, and some communities do not have any WFS, MFS, RR, or SMART groups at all.

Many areas have recovery clubs for people recovering from alcohol or drug problems. These clubs provide an atmosphere that is alcohol- and drug-free (except for cigarettes). Members can attend support group meetings and social events and interact informally with each other over a meal or cup of coffee.

It helps to have as much firsthand information as possible about various self-help programs available in the client's community. Attending meetings that are open to the public, reading the literature, and talking with others who have attended self-help programs are excellent ways for the therapist to gain knowledge of self-help programs.

Although some clients participate throughout their lives in self-help programs, others use them for only a specific period of time. Clients vary in their needs for involvement in self-help programs. Some are turned off by being told they have to maintain lifelong involvement.

As discussed in the previous chapter, some clients have high levels of social anxiety that make it difficult for them to attend meetings, talk during meetings, or initiate informal discussions with other members before, during, or after meetings. These clients may need help in challenging beliefs that prevent them from attending self-help meetings or help in learning social skills that make it easier for them to interact in group situations.

Major Points and Issues for Discussion

The following are major points and issues for discussion:

1. The therapist discusses various self-help programs, recovery clubs, or clubhouses available in the client's area. The therapist can pro-

vide brochures, written descriptions, and recommendations for books on specific programs, such as *Alcoholics Anonymous* (the "Big Book," 2001), *Narcotics Anonymous* (the "Basic Text," 1988), and *The Dual Disorders Recovery Book* (1993).

2.   Self-help programs are most effective when the client actively participates. These programs vary in their philosophy or approach to recovery, but most involve the following elements:

Fellowship. This involves people with similar problems helping each other deal with their alcohol problems, drug problems, or both. They do this by sharing experiences in and out of meetings, "sponsoring" newcomers (commonly done in AA and NA), and being available to talk about recovery issues of mutual concern, such as how to deal with cravings to use, how to recover from a lapse or relapse, or how to undo the damage inflicted on family members or other people as a result of substance use.

Recovery meetings. These involve discussing recovery issues or listening to personal stories of others who share their experiences with substance use disorders and recovery.

Program steps or guidelines. These involve particular steps a client can take to deal with the alcohol or drug problem. Programs such as the 12 steps of AA and NA are seen by many as a way of life, not just a way of overcoming a substance use disorder.

Self-help literature. Many booklets, books, and tapes are available to provide information, inspiration, or hope. Many are written by people in recovery from an alcohol or drug problem.

Social events. Some mutual support programs such as AA or NA sponsor social events such as holiday celebrations or activities. These events provide an alcohol- and drug-free environment in which recovering individuals can have fun, meet other people, and not feel pressured to use substances.

3.   The client completes the Self-Help Program Worksheet (Figure 15.1). On this worksheet the client describes what it is like to ask for help, summarizes previous experiences in self-help programs, and identifies potential drawbacks and benefits of participating in self-help groups.

Self-Help Program Worksheet

Instructions: Complete the following items to help you decide how self-help programs could help you stop using alcohol, tobacco, or other drugs and help reduce the chances or relapse.

1. Describe what it is like for you to ask others for help and support.

It's hard, I usually prefer working out my problems on my own.

2. Summarize your previous experiences in self-help programs (pro and con).

NA meetings were helpful because I learned ways to stay clean. The steps were hard, though, especially step 4. I did good until I blew off meetings and stopped completely.

3. List potential drawbacks of participating in self-help programs.

It's hard to find the time because of my work and family obligations. Some people are too intrusive. Others are phony.

4. List potential benefits of participating in self-help programs.

People are supportive, most don't judge you if you mess up, they know what works, the steps help you become a better person, and meetings are everywhere.

5. Which specific self-help program(s) do you think would benefit you in quitting or staying off alcohol, tobacco, or other drugs?

NA has worked the best for me.

Figure 15.1

Example of a completed Self-Help Program Worksheet.

4. The therapist discusses the client's beliefs and attitudes about asking others for help and attending self-help programs, recovery clubs, or clubhouses. Many clients have unrealistic ideas about how these programs work or what is expected. For example, some believe that they have to stand in front of a crowd of strangers and publicly confess that they are an alcoholic or a drug addict.

5. The therapist discusses with the client his or her previous involvement in self-help programs, recovery clubs, or clubhouses. What did the client find helpful and unhelpful? Even if a particular program was not helpful in the past, this does not mean that it cannot benefit the client at this time.

6. The therapist should be respectful of the client's negative feelings or views about self-help programs, recovery clubs, or clubhouses. If a client can articulate why a particular program was not helpful before and why he or she doesn't wish to attend, other options should be considered.

7. The therapist encourages skeptical clients to attend a certain number of self-help meetings or even meetings of different groups before they make a final decision as to whether self-help programs can help. For example, we often ask clients to attend 6 to 12 meetings before reaching a decision about the usefulness of such meetings.

8. The therapist lets the client choose from among various self-help programs, recovery clubs, or clubhouses. How does the client perceive the pros and cons of each program? The therapist needs to be aware of his or her own biases. The therapist may not agree with a particular self-help group's philosophy or program, but it is up to the client to choose which program to attend.

9. The therapist provides lists of self-help programs or names of people to contact. Some clients are comfortable choosing programs from lists, but other feel more comfortable having a name of a specific individual to call. For many, having someone specific to contact eases the transition to a self-help group.

10. The therapist encourages the client to get a list of telephone numbers of other members of self-help groups and learn to reach out for help and support. In some instances, clients need help learning social skills so that they can appropriately ask other people for support. Behavioral rehearsals can help the client feel more prepared to reach out for help from others.

11. The therapist monitors the client's attendance at self-help programs and discusses the client's reactions, especially in the early stage of recovery. For example, a client may attend only one or two meetings and declare, "The program is not for me." Another client may focus on one particular person in a group who she feels is being dishonest or hypocritical and judge the entire program based on this one individual.

12. If the client refuses to attend any self-help meetings yet is unable to reach his goals with therapy, adjunctive medications, or both, the therapist discusses with the client how another trial or self-help meeting may be beneficial.

13. Clients with significant levels of social anxiety and avoidant behavior may need specific help addressing their anxiety and avoidance before they will be ready to participate in self-help meetings. Therapists who cannot provide treatment for this type of problem should refer these clients to a professional with expertise in treating social anxiety or social phobias.

Homework for Client

■ Complete Self-Help Program Worksheet.

Assessing and Treating Co-occurring
Psychiatric Disorders

Chapter 16 *Assessment of Co-occurring Psychiatric Disorders*

(Corresponds to chapter 20 of the workbook)

Introduction

In the first section of this chapter, we review the patterns, prevalence, and effects of substance use disorders combined with psychiatric disorders (referred to as "co-occurring" or "dual" disorders). The next sections review the relationships between psychiatric and substance use disorders and eight challenges for clinicians and providers. We then discuss the process of conducting a comprehensive and thorough assessment of psychiatric and substance use disorders using the *DSM-IV* multi-axis format (APA, 2000a). We also discuss the importance of conveying assessment findings to the client and/or family. The third section covers the continuum of care, levels of care, treatment approaches, and clinical issues. The importance of therapeutic alliance between caregivers and the client is discussed, since this is one of the key variables affecting treatment outcome. The fourth section reviews the process of recovery. We then address issues related to relapse, suicide, violence, and HIV, AIDS, or hepatitis.

Prevalence, Patterns, and Effects of Co-occurring Disorders

Prevalence

Substance use disorders combined with psychiatric disorders are common clinical conditions encountered by health professionals in psychiatric and addiction medicine settings. Two large-scale epidemiological studies have documented high rates of co-occurring disorders: the Epi-

Table 16.1 Lifetime Prevalence of Common Adult Disorders

Alcohol abuse or dependence	13.7%
Phobias	12.6%
Drug abuse or dependence	6.1%
Major depression	5.1%
Antisocial personality disorder	2.5%
Obsessive-compulsive disorder	2.5%
Dysthymia	1.5%
Panic disorder	1.5%
Cognitive dysfunction	1.1%
Schizophrenia	1.0%
Mania	0.4%
Somatization	0.1%
Anorexia	0.1%

demiological Catchment Area study (ECA; Robins & Regier, 1991), and the National Comorbidity Study (ECS; Kessler et al., 1996).

The ECA study gathered data on over 20,000 subjects from five major areas in the United States. Results showed that 22.5 percent of adults in the United States met lifetime criteria for a non-substance abuse mental disorder, and 16.4 percent met lifetime criteria for an alcohol or drug use disorder. The lifetime prevalences of the more common adult disorders are listed in Table 16.1.

The ECA found that 37% of individuals with alcohol use disorders and 53% of individuals with drug use disorders met lifetime criteria for a psychiatric illness. The ECA survey also found high rates of substance use disorders among those who met criteria for these specific psychiatric disorders:

Antisocial disorders	85%
Bipolar illness	61%
Schizophrenia	47%

The NCS involved over 8,000 subjects and found that 51% of individuals with a psychiatric disorder had a substance use disorder. Depending on the substance of abuse, 41 to 66 percent of respondents had a lifetime psychiatric disorder. The NCS estimated that there are over 10 million individuals in the United States with co-occurring disorders.

Numerous clinical studies have also documented high rates of co-occurring disorders (CSAT, 2005c; Daley & Moss, 2002; Drake & Mueser, 2000; Drake et al., 1998; Mueser et al., 2003; Westermeyer, Weiss, & Ziedonis, 2003). Rates of co-occurring substance use disorders are especially high among individuals with antisocial or borderline personality disorder, bipolar illness, and schizophrenia.

Patterns

The clinical presentation and problems of a given individual will vary depending on the severity of the disorders. Clients may experience any combination of disorders with varying degrees of severity. The substance use and psychiatric disorders each may be mild, moderate, or severe. In some instances, the affected individual will have severe patterns of both types of disorders, which will complicate recovery and challenge professionals providing treatment.

Many individuals experience a single episode of a mental disorder and function well when the disorder is in remission, with no residual adverse effects. Others experience occasional episodes over time with little or no serious residual disability between episodes. However, there is a significant group of clients who experience repeated episodes with significant residual disability. These clients have persistent symptoms that are more or less present all of the time and are sometimes referred to as having serious and persistent mental illness (SPMI). Although clients with SPMI can include those from most of the *DSM-IV* diagnostic categories, many have schizophrenia, recurrent mood or anxiety disorders, or borderline personality disorder. Many SPMI clients also have comorbid substance abuse or dependency (Linehan et al., 1999; Minkoff & Drake, 1991; Montrose & Daley, 1995; Rosenthal & Westreich, 1999). These are the clients most likely to need long-term psychiatric or dual diagnosis treatment, inpatient care during periods of symptom exacerbation, and ancillary social services such as case management, housing, community residential programs, vocational training, partial hospital programs, or intensive outpatient programs.

Effects

Psychiatric and substance use disorders are associated with a range of problems in all areas of functioning for the affected client, the family, and society (Daley, Salloum, & Thase, 2000; Drake & Mueser, 2000). The specific effects on a client will depend on the type and severity of the disorder(s), personality, personal competencies, coping mechanisms, and behaviors exhibited. Areas of functioning affected include medical or physical, psychological or emotional, family, social or interpersonal, spiritual, occupational, legal, and financial status. Following are examples that illustrate the effects of co-occurring disorders:

- An alcoholic client's life is seriously jeopardized due to severe weight loss and poor nutrition associated with her anorexia.

- A client with cocaine abuse and borderline personality disorder makes multiple parasuicide or suicide gestures, creating havoc with the family and significant relationships, leading to family conflict and distress. Her behaviors also lead to feelings of rejection, which in turn contributes to her increased depression and use of cocaine.

- A drug-dependent client with problems with violence suffers physical injuries and causes serious injuries to another due to a violent altercation. His involvement in illegal activities to support an expensive drug habit increases his risk of being incarcerated.

- A recovering alcoholic client in a manic episode is convinced that he has the perfect business idea that will make him rich. He takes out a large loan and uses his family's saving account to finance his idea and subsequently loses all of the money.

- An alcoholic client misses work due to hangovers, loses a job, and seriously jeopardizes the financial stability of her family. Her erratic and unpredictable behavior when drinking causes her husband and children to worry, and her vulgar verbal attacks upset and bother her family.

- A client with marijuana abuse and schizophrenia who has poor social skills feels isolated due to difficulties interacting with others and building interpersonal relationships. She spends much of her time alone and also feels depressed.

- A recovering opiate-addicted individual with recurrent depression feels guilty and shameful about being ill and unable to function adequately as a parent. He feels a sense of "emptiness," and little in life seems meaningful or important to him besides his children. He also feels demoralized due to multiple episodes of depression over time. He is worried that he may relapse to opiate use again.

- A woman is so anxious and fearful that she can barely leave her home to buy groceries or see a doctor. She feels like a prisoner in her own house and is increasingly despondent as a result. She won't even leave to visit her adult children, who live in a nearby town.

Many studies report higher rates of problems among individuals with co-occurring disorders compared to those with only a single disorder (Daley & Moss, 2002). Drake and Mueser (2000) reviewed over 100 studies and found higher rates of the following problems among individuals with co-occurring disorders:

- Severe financial problems

- Unstable housing and homelessness

- Medication noncompliance

- Relapse to either disorder

- Use of psychiatric services, emergency room services, and hospital services

- Violence

- Legal problems

- Incarceration

- Depression and suicide

- Family burden

- Sexually transmitted disorders and HIV infection

One of the authors (D.D.) and his colleagues at the University of Pittsburgh Medical Center have documented significant differences between clients with psychiatric disorders and those who also have a co-occurring substance use disorder (Cornelius et al., 1996, 1997; Daley, Salloum, & Thase, 2000; Salloum et al., 1996; Salloum, Daley, & Thase, 2000). Compared to those who had only a psychiatric disorder, those with co-occurring disorders were found to have:

- More diagnoses, psychiatric hospitalizations, and days in the hospital

- Higher rates of psychiatric re-hospitalization

- Higher rates of suicidality

- Higher rates of homicidality

- Lower rates of treatment entry and completion

- Lower rates of successful transition from inpatient to ambulatory care

- Lower rates of ambulatory session attendance

Relationships Between Psychiatric and Substance Use Disorders

There are several possible relationships between psychiatric illness and substance use disorders (Daley & Moss, 2002; Meyer, 1986; Salloum & Thase, 2001). These include:

1. Axis I and II psychopathology serves as a risk factor for addictive disorders. The odds of having an addictive disorder among individuals with a psychiatric disorder is 2.7, according to the ECA survey.

2. Addiction is a risk factor for psychiatric illness. The odds of having a psychiatric disorder among those with a drug use disorder is

4.5, according to the ECA survey, making drug abusers 4.5 times more likely than non-drug abusers to have a psychiatric diagnosis.

3. Clients with psychiatric disorders are more vulnerable than others to the adverse effects of alcohol or other drugs. For example, the use of marijuana or hallucinogens can be much more harmful to a person with schizophrenia or borderline personality disorder than a person who does not have one of these disorders.

4. The use of drugs can precipitate an underlying psychiatric condition. For example, PCP, methamphetamine, or cocaine use may trigger a first manic episode in a vulnerable individual.

5. Psychopathology may modify the course of an addictive disorder in terms of how quickly a disorder develops, the symptoms experienced, adherence to treatment, response to treatment, and long-term outcome. Those with co-occurring disorders tend to have a worse clinical outcome than those with comorbidity (Daley & Moss, 2002; Drake et al., 1998).

6. Psychiatric symptoms can develop in the course of chronic intoxications. For example, psychosis may follow PCP use or chronic stimulant or cocaine use, or suicidality and depression may follow a cocaine crash or alcohol binge.

7. Psychiatric symptoms can emerge as a consequence of chronic use of substances or a relapse. For example, depression may be caused by an awareness of the losses associated with addiction or after a relapse.

8. Substance-using behavior and psychiatric symptoms, regardless of which came first, will become linked over the course of time.

9. The addictive disorder and the psychiatric disorder can develop at different points in time. For example, a bipolar client may become hooked on drugs years after being stable from a manic disorder; or an alcoholic may develop panic disorder or major depression long after becoming sober.

10. Symptoms of one disorder can contribute to relapse of the other disorder and the need for hospitalization. For example, an increase in anxiety or hallucinations may lead a client with schizophrenia

to alcohol or other drug use to ameliorate symptoms; a cocaine or alcohol binge may lead to depressive symptoms or suicidality.

Challenges for Clinicians and Providers

We see the following as the challenges facing clinicians and treatment systems providing care to clients with dual disorders:

1. *Convey helpful attitudes.* We have consulted with numerous professionals about their frustration and negative attitudes in dealing with psychiatrically ill clients who have substance use disorders. Anger, frustration, and judgmentalism are commonly expressed. Such negative reactions and feelings must be contained. To be effective, clinicians must understand and accept these clients as being ill and must covey genuine concern and empathy.

2. *Understand illness "from the inside out."* Try to understand what it is like to be dependent on substances, or want to use alcohol or drugs so badly that you are willing to risk losing your family, job, or health. Think about what it feels like to have a psychiatric disorder and how this affects your self-image, ability to function, or vision of the future.

3. *Develop client- and family-centered standards of care.* A panel of national experts on dual disorders developed standards of care, practice guidelines, workforce competencies, and training curricula (CMHS, 1998). This panel recommended that clinical care for clients and families should be:

   Welcoming: Services should be consumer-centered; caregivers need to show empathy towards clients and optimism about their chances for recovery, even those who struggle with motivation to change and make minimal changes.

   Accessible: Clients with any combination of disorders need to be accommodated in treatment systems, regardless of their level of readiness to change.

   Integrated: Clinicians should be competent in both mental health and substance abuse treatment approaches so that integrated care is provided.

Continuous: When possible, the treatment team should maintain continuous contact with the client throughout all episodes.

Comprehensive: Treatment services should be sensitive to cultural and gender issues and should offer a range of clinical and ancillary services to address the needs and problems of the client.

4. *Think family, not just consumer.* Families and children are adversely affected by dual disorders. Helping the client examine the impact of disorders on the family, eliciting support from the family, and providing education, support, and therapy to the family are some of the ways in which families can be helped.

5. *Provide integrated assessment and treatment services.* A comprehensive assessment takes time and effort and is used to guide treatment planning. An assessment must include a substance use, psychiatric, psychosocial, and medical history. Integrated treatment services focus on both substance use and psychiatric issues, acknowledging that each affects the other.

6. *Integrate evidence-based treatments into clinical care.* Many scientific studies have been conducted to determine the efficacy of various treatments for psychiatric illness, addiction, or dual disorders. Clinicians should be aware of evidence-based treatments and integrate these into clinical care. Our recommendation is that mental health professionals learn one model of addiction treatment and integrate appropriate interventions into their daily work. Likewise, addiction medicine professionals can learn one model of treatment for psychiatric illness and integrate this into their clinical care with dual diagnosis clients.

7. *Improve linkages between different levels of care.* Clients who fail to engage in the next level of care following completion of another level are at risk for relapse. For example, psychiatric inpatients who enter ambulatory care and adhere to an adequate dose of treatment are less likely to be rehospitalized than those who fail to continue care after hospital discharge. Many effective motivational and adherence-improvement interventions exist that can help clinicians improve these linkages (Daley & Zuckoff, 1999).

8. *Use strategies to improve adherence to treatment.* Clients benefit from treatment to the extent that they remain in it for a sufficient period of time. No short-term treatments exist for dual disorders, particularly for clients who have more serious and persistent forms of mental illness. There are many systems and clinical-related strategies that improve adherence. Clinicians should become familiar with adherence-improving strategies and integrate these into their clinical work (Daley & Zuckoff, 1999).

Types of Psychiatric Disorders

DSM-IV-TR diagnostic categories for adults include organic mental, psychoactive substance use, schizophrenic, paranoid, and other psychotic, mood (affective), anxiety, somatoform, dissociative, psychosexual, factitious, impulse control, adjustment, and personality disorders (Table 16.2). Many clients have multiple psychiatric disorders. For example, the NCS study found that almost 54% of individuals with depression experienced an anxiety disorder. Those with substance use and co-occurring psychiatric disorders often have three to five different *DSM* diagnoses excluding substance intoxication or withdrawal.

Following is a brief description of the most common psychiatric disorders found among clients with substance use disorders (APA, 2000a; Daley & Moss, 2002):

1. *Mood disorders.* These involve a disturbance of mood or prolonged emotional state that is not caused by a medical or other mental disorder (Daley, 2006; Daley & Haskett, 2003; Daley & Thase, 2003; Frank, 2005; Kupfer et al., 1992; Thase, 1999; Westermeyer, Weiss, & Ziedonis, 2003). *Major depression* involves a dysphoric mood or loss of interest or pleasure in the client's usual activities or pastimes, along with other symptoms such as poor appetite, sleep disturbance, fatigue, loss of energy, or suicidality. *Bipolar disorder* involves mania, an elevated, expansive or irritable mood accompanied by other significant symptoms such as an increase in activity, restlessness, or pressured speech. The client with a bipolar illness may experience a manic episode, depressive episode, or mixed episode. Major depression or bipolar disorders may also in-

Table 16.2 *DSM-IV-TR* Diagnostic Categories for Adults

Types of Disorders	Severity and Course Specifiers
Psychotic	Mild to severe
Mood	Partial to full remission
Anxiety	Relapse and recurrence
Somatoform	
Factitious	
Dissociative	
Sexual and gender identity	
Eating	
Sleep	
Impulse control	
Adjustment	
Personality	
Substance use	
Other conditions that may be a focus of clinical work	

Adapted from *Diagnostic and Statistical Manual of Mental Disorder, DSM IV TR, 5th ed.* (2000). Washington, DC: American Psychiatric Association.

clude psychotic features. Major depression may be experienced as a single episode or as a recurrent disorder with multiple episodes of depression over time. About one third of individuals with depression and 60% of those with bipolar illness will experience a substance use disorder. About half of individuals who experience an episode of major depression will have at least one recurrence (Kupfer et al., 1992).

2. *Anxiety disorders.* This group of disorders involves anxiety as the predominant symptom and includes phobias, panic disorder, generalized anxiety disorder, obsessive-compulsive disorder, and post-traumatic stress disorder (Antony & Swinson, 2000; Brown, Muellar, & Stout, 1999; Daley & Salloum, 2003; Foa, Keane, & Friedman, 2000; Triffleman, Carroll, & Kellogg, 1998). *Phobias* involve persistent and irrational fears of objects, activities, or situations that lead to avoidant behavior. The three major types of pho-

bias are agoraphobia, social phobia, and simple phobia. *Agoraphobia,* the most severe and pervasive form, involves a fear of being alone or in public places from which escape would be difficult. This disorder is sometimes accompanied by *panic attacks,* which involve sudden and intense periods of apprehension or fear along with physical symptoms such as heart palpitations, dizziness, sweating, shaking, or trembling. A *social phobia* involves a persistent and irrational fear of, and a desire to avoid, a situation where the person is worried about being scrutinized by others (e.g., speaking or eating in front of others). The person also is afraid that he or she may act in a way that is humiliating or embarrassing. A *simple phobia* is a persistent or irrational desire to avoid objects (e.g., certain animals) or situations (e.g., closed spaces, heights, or flying in an airplane). A *generalized anxiety disorder* involves persistent anxiety along with symptoms of motor tension (e.g., shakiness, trembling, trouble relaxing), autonomic hyperactivity (e.g., pounding heart, dizziness, upset stomach), apprehension (e.g., anxiety, worry, or fear in anticipating some misfortune will occur), and vigilance and scanning (e.g., feeling on edge). An *obsessive-compulsive disorder* involves obsessions and/or compulsions that are distressing and interfere with the person's ability to function. *Post-traumatic stress disorder* involves the reexperiencing of a psychologically traumatic event (e.g., rape, assault, combat, accident, or natural disaster) through recurrent dreams or recollections of the event, along with a numbing of responsiveness or reduced involvement with the world. Co-occurring substance use disorders are high among all types of anxiety disorders.

3. *Schizophrenia.* Numerous studies and clinical writings have reported high rates of substance use disorders among individuals with schizophrenia (Bellack & DiClemente, 1999; Daley & Montrose, 2003; Montrose & Daley, 1995; Mueser et al., 2003). This mental disorder involves psychotic symptoms (e.g., hallucinations) and disturbances in thinking (e.g., delusions, illogical thinking, loose associations), inappropriate or flat affect, sense of self, goal-directed activity, interpersonal relationships, and psychomotor behavior that contribute to a significant deterioration in routine functioning. This disorder represents one of the most chronic and

potentially debilitating categories of psychiatric illness, as many schizophrenics experience a lifelong course of the illness.

4. *Eating disorders (anorexia and bulimia).* These are characterized by gross disturbances in eating behavior (Marcus & Levia, 2001). In *anorexia*, the person has an intense fear of becoming obese and a disturbed body image, loses a significant amount of weight, and refuses to maintain a normal body weight. *Bulimia* involves recurrent episodes of binge eating followed by depressed mood and self-deprecating thoughts about the binges. Self-induced vomiting, restrictive diets, and diuretics may be used in attempts to lose weight.

5. *Borderline and antisocial personality disorders.* Personality disorders involve a long-term pattern of experience and behavior that deviates from what is normal in the person's culture (APA, 2000a; Cloninger & Svrakic, 2000; Gunderson & Gabbard, 2000; Livesley, 2001). This pattern is manifested in a variety of personal and social situations and causes significant personal distress or impairment in functioning. The person has a distorted way of viewing himself or herself, others, and the world; problems with emotional responses; poor impulse control; and/or significant relationship problems. A *borderline personality disorder* (BPD) involves unstable and intense relationships; impulsiveness; emotional lability; inappropriate and intense anger or problems controlling anger; recurrent suicidal threats, gestures, or behaviors or self-mutilating behaviors; identity disturbance; chronic emptiness; and frantic efforts to avoid abandonment. Some individuals with BPD experience psychotic symptoms. This disorder is much more common among women than men and is associated with other types of psychiatric and substance use disorders (Koerner & Linehan, 2000; Linehan, 1993). About two thirds of individuals with BPD will also experience a substance use disorder.

6. *Antisocial personality disorder* (ASP) involves a pattern of antisocial behavior in which the rights of others are violated. The person with ASP often breaks the law, deceives others, lacks remorse for behaviors, and is irresponsible and impulsive. ASP is much more common among men than women, and the majority of individu-

als with this disorder also have problems with alcohol or drug abuse. Most individuals with ASP (85%) experience a substance use disorder.

Causes of Psychiatric Disorders

Psychiatric disorders are caused by interacting biological, psychological, and social-cultural (environmental) factors (Andreasen, 2001; Sadock & Sadock, 2000; Stein, Kupfer, & Schatzberg, 2006; Torrey, 2001; Torrey & Knable, 2002). The biopsychosocial framework is a widely used paradigm for understanding psychiatric disorders, as it considers multiple interacting causal factors in the development of an initial or recurrent episode of illness. The degree of influence of each of these major elements depends on the specific type of disorder, as some disorders may have more of a genetic vulnerability and biological component than others.

1. *Biological.* These include diseases; genetic vulnerability; dysregulations in dopamine, norepinephrine, serotonin, acetylcholine, and gamma-aminobutyric acid systems; and differences in brain structure. Many mood, anxiety, psychotic, and addictive disorders run in families, increasing the risk to offspring or first-degree relatives. The relative risk of acquiring a specific disorder is higher than that of chance.

2. *Psychological.* These include attitudes and beliefs, psychological defenses, coping skills, problem-solving abilities, and personality factors. For example, studies show that there were often early childhood personality indicators (e.g., higher levels of aggressiveness and affective expressiveness) among children of bipolar parents (Miklowitz & Goldstein, 1997).

3. *Social-cultural.* These include early experiences within the family and one's culture, environmental influences, and level of social support. On the other hand, there are also "protective" factors such as a supportive family or social environment that may reduce vulnerability to mental or substance use disorders among some individuals.

Multiple methods are used to gather information during the assessment process in order to determine psychiatric diagnoses and make treatment recommendations according to five axes. These methods include clinical interviews and observations of the client, review of previous records (treatment, medical, psychological test results) or laboratory tests, collateral interviews (family, significant others, other caregivers, or social service professionals), and the use of pen-and-paper questionnaires that elicit information about specific disorders such as depression or social phobia.

The assessment process can be complicated when the client is psychotic, intoxicated, or uncooperative; denies or minimizes psychiatric symptoms; or has no motivation or interest in being helped. An assessment may take one or more sessions, depending on the client's condition and the complexity of the situation. A client may have multiple psychiatric, substance use, personality, or medical diagnoses as well as multiple social problems or significant stressors.

Provisional, or "rule-out," diagnoses can be given in cases in which it is not clear if an actual *DSM* disorder is present and more information is needed. For example, a client with alcohol dependence may have symptoms of depression. The clinical history may show that this client never suffered major depression when not drinking, and that he has been drinking heavily during the entire current episode of depression. A provisional diagnosis may be given until it can be determined if clinical depression exists in the absence of active symptoms of alcohol dependence. In the absence of a clear-cut prior history of major depression, this particular case would require that the client be abstinent from alcohol for a period of time, usually several weeks or longer, before it can be determined if a major depression exists.

The *DSM* multi-axis format provides a comprehensive approach to assessment of the client on five axes (APA, 2000a) (Table 16.3):

1. *Axis I: Clinical disorders.* These include schizophrenia and other psychotic, mood, anxiety, somatoform, factitious, dissociative, sexual and gender identity, eating, sleep, impulse control, and adjustment disorders. Each specific disorder has a cluster of symptoms (physical, emotional, behavioral, cognitive), time requirements, and functioning impairments associated with it.

Table 16.3 *DSM-IV-TR* Multiaxial Formulation for Mental and Substance Use Disorders

Axis I: Clinical Disorders

- Substance use, mood, anxiety, somatoform, factitious, dissociative, sexual and gender identity, eating, sleep impulse control and adjustment disorders

Axis II: Personality Disorders

- Prominent maladaptive personality features or defense mechanisms
- Mental Retardation

Axis III: General Medical Conditions

Axis IV: Psychosocial and Environmental Problems

- Primary support groups
- Social environment
- Educational
- Occupational
- Housing
- Economic
- Access to health care
- Legal
- Other problems

Axis V: Global Assessment of Functioning

Adapted from *Diagnostic and Statistical Manual of Mental Disorder, DSM-IV-TR, 5th ed. (2000). Washington, DC: American Psychiatric Association.*

2. *Axis II: Personality disorders and mental retardation.* These include paranoid, schizoid, schizotypal, antisocial, borderline, histrionic, narcissistic, avoidant, dependent, obsessive-compulsive, and personality disorder not otherwise specified. Even if the client does not meet full criteria for a personality disorder, the clinician can note significant "traits" on Axis II (e.g., antisocial, narcissistic, paranoid).

3. *Axis III: General medical conditions and disorders.* These include any condition, disorder, or disease caused by injury, poisoning, or infection; associated with pregnancy, childbirth, or the postpartum period; or involving the nervous system, blood, sense organs, skin, or any of the major systems (circulatory, respiratory, digestive, genitourinary, musculoskeletal). These conditions or disorders

may be etiologically significant to the primary mental disorder. Or, an Axis III condition may not be etiologically significant but may have implications for the management of the mental or substance use disorders.

4. *Axis IV: Psychosocial and environmental problems.* These include problems with the primary support group or social environment, education, occupation, housing, economic status, access to healthcare, crime, and the legal system. These problems may contribute to the exacerbation of the current disorder or result from it. Axis IV is also coded for severity (e.g., none, minimal, mild, moderate, severe, extreme).

5. *Axis V: Global assessment of functioning (current and past year).* This is the clinician's judgment of the client's current overall level of functioning and highest level of functioning within the past year related to interpersonal relationships, occupation, and use of leisure time. Level of functioning includes superior, very good, good, fair, poor, very poor, and grossly impaired.

As part of the comprehensive psychiatric assessment, the clinician includes current or past suicidal ideation or behavior; aggressive ideation or behavior; drug or alcohol use; developmental and social history; significant family history of medical, psychiatric, and substance use disorders; level of motivation; impact of disorders on self and others; and client strengths or personal resources. A mental status examination is also performed to assess orientation, attention and calculation, recall, and language.

Psychiatric illness is a significant problem among many individuals who have substance use disorders and has major implications for their recovery and for the development of the initial treatment plan. The presence of any type of psychiatric illness can complicate the assessment and treatment of a substance use disorder. Therefore, a psychiatric history should be gathered to document current and past psychiatric symptoms and disorders, effects of illness on the client and significant others, treatment, and motivation to change.

Findings of the psychiatric assessment are used to establish diagnoses, including provisional ones, using Axes I through V; to determine recommendations for further evaluation; to discuss treatment options with the client; and to make an initial agreement on the treatment plan and disposition. In the current climate of managed care, in which treatment services have to be authorized and are subject to review, thorough assessments are all the more important to justify both initial treatment recommendations and ongoing treatment.

Conveying Assessment Findings to the Client and Family

Once a psychiatric assessment is complete, the clinician can review the findings with the client to present the diagnosis and the clinical information upon which it is based. If the client meets criteria for a specific *DSM-IV-TR* disorder, the symptoms and associated behaviors can be reviewed in specific detail to identify the disorder for the client. This process often leads to discussion of the etiology of the disorder, what the client thinks and feels about the diagnosis, and the recommendations for treatment. Clients who deny or minimize their disorder can be helped to accept it through this process of sharing findings of the assessment. If the family is involved in the assessment process, they can also be involved in this feedback process so that they can share their reactions to the information presented and ask questions about the disorder or treatment.

In some instances, the client will have some symptoms of a mental health disorder but not meet full criteria of the diagnosis. These are sometimes referred to as "subsyndromal" disorders.

Getting the Client to Accept Help

Common Barriers to Seeking Treatment

Some clients willingly accept recommendations for treatment of a psychiatric disorder. However, many do not seek treatment despite the serious nature of their psychiatric problems. They refuse treatment recommendations, accept them but then fail to follow through with the treatment referral, drop out of treatment prematurely, or comply poorly with the treatment plan. They may, for example, miss treatment sessions, fail to take medications as prescribed, or not follow other specific recommendations made by the treating professional. Resistance is common, and caregivers need to understand the factors affecting the client's motivation to engage in treatment and to determine how to lower resistance so that the client follows through with the treatment referral.

Table 16.4 summarizes the major factors affecting a client's adherence to the recommendations of a professional to get help for a mental health, substance use, or dual disorder (Daley & Zuckoff, 1999). These include client-related factors, illness- or symptom-related factors, relationship and social support variables, and treatment systems variables. Usually a com-

Table 16.4 Factors Affecting Client Adherence With Treatment Recommendations

Client Variables	Illness & Symptom Related Variables	Relationship & Social Support Variables	Treatment & System Variables
Motivation	Symptoms of addiction	Negative social supports	Therapeutic alliance
Beliefs	Symptoms of psychiatric illness	Unstable living situation	Friendliness of treatment staff
Stigma	Obsessions or cravings to use	Poverty	Competence of staff
Expectations	Social anxiety	Homelessness	Demands on counselor
Satisfaction with treatment	Previous history of illness and relapse		Supervision of staff
Personality	Failure to catch early warning signs of relapse		Access to treatment
Other addictions (gambling, smoking, etc.)	Improvement in symptoms or problems		Characteristics of treatment setting
Other life events or problems			Type of treatment offered
			Duration of treatment
			Intensity of treatment
			Appropriateness of treatment recommendations
			Medication problems
			Expense of treatment
			Ineffective treatment
			Continuity of care
			Availability of other services

Adapted from Daley, DC & Zuckoff, A. *Improving Treatment Compliance: Counseling and Systems Strategies for Substance Abuse and Dual Disorders.* Center City, MN: Hazelden, 1999 p. 40.

Table 16.5 Clinical Strategies to Improve Adherence

Therapeutic Relationship

- Express empathy and concern.
- Convey helpfulness in attitudes and behaviors.
- Encourage discussions of the counseling process.
- Encourage discussions of client-counselor relationship.

Motivation

- Accept ambivalence as normal.
- Accept and appreciate small changes.
- Accept varying levels of readiness to change.
- Anticipate noncompliance at various stages of treatment.
- Discuss prior history of compliance.
- Discuss current compliance problems immediately.

Treatment Preparation

- Provide aftercare counseling prior to discharge from residential or inpatient care.
- Help the client anticipate roadblocks to change.
- Explore expectations and hopes for treatment.

Treatment Plan Development

- Negotiate rather than dictate change plans.
- Emphasize responsibility to the client.
- Regularly review treatment goals and progress.
- Discuss pros and cons of treatment.
- Discuss pros and cons of self-help groups.
- Discuss pros and cons of abstinence.
- Provide options regarding treatment.

Treatment Process and Strategies

- Provide interventions based on empirical support.
- Change treatment frequency and intensity as needed.
- Provide direct feedback to client.
- Discuss client's reaction to feedback.
- Provide reinforcement for treatment compliance.
- Provide reinforcement for compliance with abstinence.
- Address social anxiety about treatment groups or self-help groups.
- Provide education to the client and family.
- Elicit family support and involvement.

Symptom Monitoring: Psychiatric Disorders

- Monitor psychiatric symptoms.
- Address persistent or residual psychiatric symptoms.
- Monitor psychiatric relapse warning signs.

Symptom Monitoring: Substance Use Disorders

- Monitor substance use recovery issues.
- Monitor cravings and thoughts of using substances.
- Monitor people, places and events and close calls.
- Focus on client's motivation.
- Monitor substance use relapse warning signs.

Medications

- Discuss medication for mental or substance use disorders.
- Prepare client for taking medications.
- Monitor medication compliance.
- Elicit agreement to not stop medicines without discussing with caregiver.
- Address adverse side effects of lack of efficacy of medications.
- Facilitate medication changes for ineffective medicines.
- Facilitate augmentation therapy.
- Prepare for negative reactions to medications, of self-help members.
- Discuss potential interventions between alcohol or illicit drug use, and medicines used for psychiatric or mental disorders.

Adapted from Daley, DC & Zuckoff, A. *Improving Treatment Compliance: Counseling and Systems Strategies for Substance Abuse and Dual Disorders.* Center City, MN: Hazelden, 1999, p. 83.

bination of factors has an adverse impact on a client's willingness to engage in treatment. Awareness of these common internal and external barriers to seeking help can help the professional develop strategies to increase treatment compliance.

How to Facilitate Referrals for Psychiatric Treatment

There are a number of strategies that the clinician can use to increase the odds of a client following through with specific recommendations for treatment of psychiatric illness if the clinician or his or her agency is unable to provide this service. Table 16.5 summarizes clinical strategies and Table 16.6 summarizes systems strategies that can improve the client's adherence with the treatment referral and ongoing participation.

Table 16.6 Systems Strategies That Improve Adherence

- Develop a clinic philosophy on compliance.
- Encourage staff training on motivational and compliance counseling.
- Provide easy access to treatment.
- Offer flexible appointment times.
- Offer consistent appointment times.
- Call and remind clients of the initial evaluation session.
- Call clients who fail to show for the initial evaluation.
- Call clients or family members prior to regularly scheduled treatment sessions.
- Use prompts to remind clients of scheduled sessions.
- Use written compliance contracts.
- Use creative ways of scheduling treatment appointments.
- Outreach to poorly compliant clients.
- Encourage treatment dropouts to return for services.
- Determine the reasons for poor compliance or early treatment drop out.
- Use case management services.
- Help the client access other services.
- Contact client to make sure referrals were followed up.
- Provide assistance with practical problems.
- Establish clinic and counselor thresholds for acceptable levels of treatment.

Compliance or Completion

- Conduct regular client and family satisfaction surveys.
- Continuously seek quality improvement.
- Offer integrated treatment for clients with dual disorders.

Adapted from Daley, DC & Zuckoff, A. *Improving Treatment Compliance: Counseling and Systems Strategies for Substance Abuse and Dual Disorders.* Center City, MN: Hazelden, 1999, p. 100.

Homework for Client

▓ Complete the Assessing Your Psychiatric Symptoms Worksheet.

Chapter 17   *Treatment of Co-occurring Psychiatric Disorders*

(Corresponds to chapter 20 of workbook)

Introduction

Effective intervention with clients with substance use disorders who have co-occurring psychiatric disorders requires that the clinician be conversant with the continuum of care for all disorders, as well as integrated treatment approaches. Professionals also need strategies to increase client motivation for treatment in order to facilitate acceptance of, and adherence to, referrals for treatment.

There are three paradigms for understanding and treating dual disorders: parallel, sequential, and integrated (Minkoff & Drake, 1991).

The *parallel* model involves the client receiving treatment for the psychiatric disorder in a mental health program and treatment for the substance use disorder in an addiction medicine program. Involvement in separate agencies increases the odds of poor adherence because the client has to adjust to two treatment philosophies, develop relationships with several professionals, and attend services at different locations. It is not unusual, for example, for treatment philosophies and expectations to vary between the mental health and the addiction medicine treatment agencies.

The *sequential* model involves addressing and stabilizing the most acute disorder first, then addressing the other disorder. Since symptoms often overlap and it is not easy to distinguish between primary and secondary disorders, this approach may put the client in a situation where specific symptoms are not sufficiently addressed. For example, a dual diagnosis client with depression who is receiving services from an addiction medicine program could be in a situation where the depression is seen as secondary and not addressed, thus causing undue suffering on the part of the client.

The *integrated* model is viewed as the most effective of the three models. While all three approaches may be helpful for a specific client, evidence suggests that clients receiving integrated treatment have higher rates of treatment adherence and improved clinical outcomes compared to those receiving parallel or sequential treatment, particularly clients with more persistent and chronic forms of mental illness (Mueser et al., 2003).

Treatment Approaches and Models

There are many effective treatments for clients with psychiatric disorders, including those with co-occurring substance use disorders. Individual, group, family, and somatic treatments (i.e., pharmacotherapy or electro-convulsive therapy [ECT]) are the treatment approaches used with psychiatric disorders. In addition, "programs" such as psychiatric rehabilitation or a dual diagnosis rehabilitation may be used.

We suggest that clinicians become familiar with one model of treatment and integrate this into their work with clients who have co-occurring disorders. Following is a brief list of treatment models used with psychiatric or co-occurring disorders:

- Cognitive and behavioral therapies including social skills for mood, anxiety, eating, and personality disorders (Antony & Swinson, 2000; Basco & Rush, 1996; Beck, 1976; Beck et al., 2004; Bellack et al., 2004; Foa, Keane, & Friedman, 2000; Stein, 2004)

- Dialectical behavior therapy for borderline personality disorders (Koerner & Linehan, 2000; Linehan, 1993)

- Dual disorders treatment approaches (CSAT, 2005c; Daley & Moss, 2002; Daley & Thase, 2004; Drake & Mueser, 2000; Mueser et al., 2003; Roberts, Shaner, & Eckman, 1999)

- Family and marital therapies (Miklowitz & Goldstein, 1997; Mueser & Glynn, 1999)

- Interpersonal psychotherapy for mood and other disorders (Frank, 2005; Weissman, Markowitz, & Klerman, 2000)

- Personal therapy for schizophrenia (Hogarty, 2002)

Clinicians should be familiar with "combined" approaches that involve both psychological and pharmacologic approaches, since many clients with co-occurring disorders have chronic and severe mental disorders and require medication. There is a significant literature documenting the need for combined approaches for many clients with psychiatric disorders, including those with co-occurring substance use disorders (Daley & Moss, 2002; Hoffman & Tompson, 2002; Sammons & Schmidt, 2001).

Familiarity with "integrated" treatment for co-occurring disorders is essential, given the high rates of psychiatric illness among clients with substance use disorders. Integrated treatment is best provided by a team within a dual disorders or co-occurring disorders program who can address all of the client's disorders rather than send the client to different systems of care for each type of disorder (note: there may be times in which treatment in an addiction medicine or psychiatric setting may be appropriate). Such treatment, when provided to more chronically and persistently mentally ill clients, occurs over the long term (Drake et al., 1998).

Some of the specific issues to consider assessing and addressing in treating co-occurring disorders include:

- Determining the appropriate level of care for the client

- Providing recovery-oriented treatment

- Facilitating treatment entry and adherence

- Evaluating the impact of the disorders on the family and helping the family

- Reducing the risk of recurrence of psychiatric illness

- Assessing and reducing suicide risk

- Assessing and reducing the risk of violence

Determining the Appropriate Level of Care

The continuum of care for psychiatric disorders, from the most to the least restrictive level, involves the following treatment settings and services (Daley & Salloum, 2001). Treatment settings and services that focus on both substance use and psychiatric issues are recommended as the first choice.

1. *Long-term psychiatric hospitalization.* This is for the more persistently and chronically mentally ill client who continues to evidence serious psychiatric symptoms, impairment in functioning, and an inability to function in the community due to the serious threat of harm to self or others. Long-term care focuses on treating symptoms, improving coping skills, and preparing clients for the community. Length of stay varies from weeks to months or longer. In recent years, there has been a decrease in the number of long-term hospital beds, with more clients returned to their community after brief periods of hospitalization. Substantial numbers of these clients have co-occurring substance use disorders and hence need services that focus on their substance use disorder in addition to their psychiatric disorders.

2. *Community residential programs.* Some chronically impaired clients need to live in supervised residential programs in order to function outside of a hospital setting. Many of these programs have on-site mental health treatment services, but in some cases clients attend day hospital programs. They receive social support and supervision in the residential facility and clinical care at a local mental health or dual diagnosis treatment program.

3. *Acute-care psychiatric hospital.* These are short-term programs (days to a few weeks) that aim to establish current diagnoses, stabilize acute symptoms of the co-occurring disorders, and develop an ongoing treatment plan for continued care. Chronic clients may have episodic admissions during periods of psychiatric symptom exacerbation, which at times may be caused or worsened by relapse to substance use following a period of sobriety. Individual, family, group, and milieu therapies; aftercare planning; and pharmacotherapy assessment and management are provided during the acute care stay. Clients usually attend mutual support groups such as AA or NA. In addition, some clients may receive ECT if they are unable to take medications or do not benefit enough from psychiatric medicine (Fink, 1999).

4. *Twenty-three-hour bed.* This service allows the treatment team to observe the client over an extended period of time to determine if an inpatient admission is needed or if the client can be better served by referral to an ambulatory program (e.g., partial hospital or outpatient care). Since the acute effects of substances also affect psychiatric symptoms and behaviors, a 23-hour bed provides time to assess whether current symptoms may be caused by alcohol or other drug use rather than the psychiatric illness.

5. *Ambulatory care: partial hospital or day program.* This program is used to divert a potential inpatient admission, as a "step-down" program for discharged inpatients, or for clients with more severe levels of symptoms and impairment who need a structured program with frequent clinical contact. Acute care programs last up to several weeks, and long-term programs last up to several months. A day in a partial hospital program includes participation in a variety of treatment groups. Individual therapy, family sessions, medication management, and/or vocational training may also be provided.

6. *Ambulatory care: outpatient or aftercare programs.* These programs are used by higher-functioning clients who do not need high levels of care and by chronically impaired clients who need follow-up care after treatment in a hospital or partial hospital program. Intensive outpatient programs may involve several treatment sessions per week. Stable clients in the maintenance phase of care may be seen only every several months. Individual, group, and family sessions and medication management are the main treatments offered in outpatient and aftercare programs. Some clients may also receive ECT as an outpatient.

7. *Other services.* Some clients may need to be detoxified while an inpatient or partial hospital client. Or, they may participate in "dual diagnosis" programs as part of their psychiatric care. Chronic psychiatric clients also benefit from intensive case management, social work services, vocational assessment and counseling, neuropsychological assessments, chaplain services, leisure counseling, and participation in self-help programs for psychiatric illness.

Recovery from co-occurring disorders refers to the process of change over time (Daley, Salloum, & Thase, 2003). Recovery tasks for clients and the skills needed to meet the challenges of recovery will depend on the stage or phase of recovery of each client. Interventions by clinicians should take into consideration the client's stage of change. For example, for some clients who have limited motivation to address their co-occurring disorders, the initial therapeutic work may focus on helping them become motivated to engage in treatment and a recovery process. Or, the focus may be on helping to stabilize the client from the most pressing acute symptoms of illness. For other clients who are more stable in their recovery, the focus of treatment may be on reducing the risk of relapse or recurrence or helping them pursue life goals related to relationships, school, work, or spirituality. Table 17.1 lists issues in recovery from co-occurring disorders in various domains: physical, psychological, behavioral, cognitive, family, interpersonal, social, and personal growth. The specific focus for each client depends on his or her current symptoms and disorders, motivation to change, internal psychological resources or coping skills, and social supports. While professional treatment can facilitate engagement in a recovery process, much of the work is done between sessions or after finishing formal treatment. Involvement in support groups for substance use or psychiatric or dual disorders provides a mechanism to help clients continue to work on their specific recovery issues.

Facilitating Treatment Entry and Adherence

There are a number of clinical strategies that can improve the client's adherence with a treatment referral (Daley et al., 1998; Daley, Salloum & Thase, 2000; Daley & Zuckoff, 1999; Miller & Rollnick, 2002). These include the following:

- Being aware of the client's motivation to enter treatment, accepting ambivalence or resistance to change, and discussing the client's questions and concerns regarding the referral

- Providing a rationale for the referral, relating the treatment recommendation to the client's current problems and concerns

Table 17.1 Issues in Recovery From Substance Use and Co-occurring Psychiatric Disorders

Physical/Lifestyle

- Exercise
- Follow a healthy diet
- Rest and relaxation
- Take medications (if needed)
- Take care of medical problem
- Learn to structure time
- Engage in pleasant activities
- Achieve balance in life

Psychological

- Monitor moods
- Manage negative moods
- Reduce anxiety
- Reduce boredom and emptiness
- Reduce guilt and shame
- Control anger/rage
- Address "losses" (grief)

Personal Growth/Maintenance

- Address spirituality issues
- Engage in meditation
- Develop relapse prevention plan for all disorders or problems
- Develop relapse interruption plan for all disorders or problems
- Use "recovery tools" on ongoing basis

Behavioral/Cognitive

- Accept the disorder(s) or problem(s)
- Control urges to drink alcohol or use drugs
- Change unhealthy beliefs and thoughts
- Reduce depressed thoughts
- Increase pleasant thoughts
- Reduce violent thoughts
- Control violent impulses
- Develop motivation to change
- Change self-defeating patterns of behavior

Family/Interpersonal/Social

- Identify effects on family and significant relationships
- Involve family in treatment/recovery
- Resolve family/marital conflicts
- Make amends to family or other significant people harmed
- Manage high risk people, places, and events
- Engage in non-drinking activities or healthy leisure interests
- Address relationship problems or deficits
- Resist social pressures to drink alcohol or use other drugs
- Resolve work, school, financial, legal problems
- Learn to face vs. avoid interpersonal conflicts
- Learn to ask for help and support
- Seek and use an AA or NA sponsor

Adapted from Daley, DC (2003). *Coping with Dual Disorders,* 2nd ed. Center City, MN: Hazelden, pp.44–45.

- ▦ Providing an orientation to the service or program to which the client is being referred (i.e., "role induction" to treatment)

- ▦ Providing a motivational session prior to referral

- ▦ Using "prompts" (phone calls or letters) prior to the initial appointment

- Engaging the family as an ally in treatment to support the client's entry into treatment

- Making a follow-up call to the client to determine if the referral was completed; helping the client who failed to follow through re-engage in treatment

In recent years, motivational strategies have been used to improve adherence rates for clients entering treatment or moving from one level of care to another (e.g., inpatient to outpatient care). These strategies have been successful with a variety of mental and substance use disorders. Even a single motivational session can have a positive impact on increasing treatment adherence.

Family Issues

Families are affected by a mental, substance use, or combination of disorders (Daley & Miller, 2001; Daley & Moss, 2002; Daley & Sinberg-Spear, 2003; Miklowitz & Goldstein, 1997; Mueser & Glynn, 1999). The family system, as well as individual members, may experience any number of adverse effects from exposure to clients, particularly those who display low motivation to change; poor judgment; or violent, suicidal, homicidal, intoxicated, bizarre, or unpredictable behavior; or those whose functioning is severely impaired. Any area of functioning of the family member—physical, emotional, social, interpersonal, occupational, spiritual, or financial—can be affected. The burden on the family can be great, and some members may even experience their own mental disorders, such as depression or anxiety, or abuse substances.

Family involvement in assessment and treatment is helpful to both the client and the family. The family can provide important assessment information, influence the client to adhere to the treatment plan, and provide support during the client's recovery. The family can also become educated about the illness, learning what they can and cannot do to help the client, and what they can do to deal with their own emotional or personal reactions (e.g., anxiety and worry, fear, anger). Family psychoeducational programs and various forms of marital and family therapy are beneficial to families and clients.

Relapse and Recurrence of Illness

All clients with mental or substance use disorders face the possibility of a relapse or recurrence of illness after a period of recovery or significantly improved functioning (Daley, 2003b; Daley & Marlatt, 2005; Marlatt & Donovan, 2005). A major focus of treatment of substance use and/or psychiatric disorders is helping clients anticipate and prepare for the possibility of relapse by learning how to identify and manage obvious and subtle signs of relapse and to identify and manage high-risk factors that increase relapse risk. Clients are also taught how to intervene early in the relapse process should it occur in order to minimize the adverse effects of a relapse and to stabilize symptoms. The more chronic and persistent forms of disorders often involve multiple episodes over time.

Facilitating Participation in Mutual Support Programs

Mutual support programs are helpful recovery resources for many clients with substance use, psychiatric, or co-occurring disorders. These include (a) programs for substance use disorders such as AA, NA, Rational Recovery, SMART Recovery, and Women for Sobriety; (b) programs for mental health problems such as Recovery, Inc., Emotional Health Anonymous, or Emotions Anonymous or programs for specific types of mental disorders such as a mood disorder or schizophrenia; and (c) programs for clients with comorbid psychiatric and substance use disorders such as Dual Recovery Anonymous, Double Trouble, or special groups within AA or NA. Self-help programs help the client learn valuable information, adopt positive recovery attitudes, learn skills to manage the illness, provide ongoing social support from others with similar problems, and provide "mentors" who can help the client use the specific "tools" of the self-help program. As managed care limits the number of treatment sessions, self-help programs are all the more important in helping clients recover from mental and substance use disorders.

Clinicians can facilitate the use of self-help programs by:

- Educating the client about the purpose and structure of the specific self-help program to which he or she is being encouraged to participate. Providing brochures, written information, and meeting lists can aid in this process.

- Discussing and acknowledging the client's resistances, questions, or concerns regarding self-help programs

- Helping to correct misconceptions that the client may have about self-help programs (e.g., you have to stand up and tell your life story to a bunch of strangers, these programs are run by religious fanatics)

- Helping the client overcome reluctance or social anxiety to attend self-help group programs. Our research shows that about one third of clients have very high levels of social anxiety and often avoid group situations as a result.

- Discussing potential ways in which a self-help program can aid the client's recovery

- Providing specific recommendations regarding a type of self-help program or particular meetings

- Negotiating an agreement in which the client will attend a certain number of meetings before making a judgment about the potential usefulness of the self-help program

- Linking the client with members of self-help programs who volunteer to help newcomers become acclimated into the programs. Some clients are more likely to attend a self-help program if they do not go alone.

- Monitoring participation and discussing both positive and negative experiences of the client who attends meetings.

Suicide

Suicide is a serious risk for some clients with substance use, psychiatric, or co-occurring disorders (Bongar, 2002; Bongar et al., 1998; Cornelius et al., 1996; Shea, 1999). Rates of suicide are highest among clients with affective disorders, schizophrenia, and alcoholism. Depression and alcoholism are the leading causes of completed suicide, with lifetime rates that are significantly higher than the general population. Having a co-morbid substance use disorder increases suicide risk even further. The risk of completion of suicide increases when more violent means are used, such as a gun. Following are some of the more common risk factors associated with suicide:

- Depression with feelings of hopelessness
- Recent heavy drinking
- Suicide threats or gestures
- Prior attempts or multiple attempts
- Suicide within the family
- Lack of social support
- Unemployment
- Living alone
- Presence of a serious medical problem or chronic illness
- Poor coping skills

Suicidal behaviors are one of the leading causes of psychiatric hospitalization. Clients with a plan or intent who are unable to guarantee their safety should be hospitalized to provide safety until there is no longer intent or a specific plan. Eliciting family support, helping the client through the crisis precipitating suicidal feelings through extra telephone contact or treatment sessions, encouraging abstinence from alcohol or other drugs, using medications to treat depressive and other psychiatric syndromes contributing to suicidality, and using an anti-suicide contract are interventions that can reduce the likelihood that the client will act on suicidal thoughts or feelings.

Violence

Violence is also a significant problem for some individuals with a mental health, substance use, or co-occurring disorder (Salloum, Daley, & Thase, 2000; Stoff, Breiling, & Maser, 1997; Swartz et al., 1998). Violence manifests in many ways, including child abuse, spouse abuse, elder abuse, sexual abuse, assault, and homicide. Often, the client who is violent in one area evidences violence in another area. Diagnoses that increase the risk of violence include:

- Schizophrenia, paranoid type

- Bipolar disorder

- Major depression

- Intermittent explosive disorder

- Post-traumatic stress disorder

- Cluster B personality disorders: especially antisocial, borderline, and narcissistic personality disorders

- Substance use, especially alcohol abuse; stimulant intoxication; hallucinogens; phencyclidine, inhalants, and other depressants

- Conduct disorders and attention deficit disorders

- Delirium, dementia, mental retardation, and seizure disorders

Treatment can help the client change beliefs, control violent impulses, and learn to manage feelings and problems without acting out in violent ways toward others. For example, men who abused their spouse and believed they were justified or wronged or the spouse deserved the abuse have to alter these beliefs in order to help them gain control over violent behaviors. These men often need help in identifying triggers to acting out, containing negative affect, and learning cognitive and behavioral skills to manage their feelings and negotiate interpersonal conflicts. Medications such as SSRI antidepressants, mood stabilizers, antipsychotics, and anxiolytics may also be used as part of the treatment approach when violence is a significant problem (Karper & Krystal, 1997).

HIV/AIDS and Hepatitis C

Dramatic medical advances over the past decade have transformed HIV infection from a short-term, inevitably fatal disease to a chronic condition amenable to treatment, similar to diabetes or congestive heart failure. However, experience has shown that both HIV infection and its treatment have neurologic and psychiatric consequences. Among barriers to successful treatment are psychiatric and substance use disorders that may place the clients at risk for infection in the first place; contribute to the spread of infection by influencing high-risk behaviors such as unprotected sex and sharing needles and equipment; and compromise adherence to antiretroviral medications. The triple diagnosis of HIV infection with a substance use disorder and a psychiatric illness has emerged as a clinical condition creating a unique set of medical and psychosocial challenges. Signs and symptoms of drug addiction, HIV, and other infections or medical diseases, psychiatric disorders, and side effects from antiretroviral medications often overlap, complicating surveillance and early identification efforts, as well as care. Clients with HIV and comorbid psychiatric disorders such as major depressive disorders and anxiety disorders require more time, effort, and resources that do other HIV-infected patients. Depression is one of the most common psychiatric disorders observed among HIV-positive individuals (Lyketsos et al., 1996). This underscores the need for interventions that reduce depression and influence HIV disease progression. Clinicians need to understand the importance of integrating treatment addressing substance abuse and mental health issues and collaborating with HIV treatment providers (Douaihy et al., 2003). Integrated care improves outcomes and quality of life.

Clients with a history of serious mental illness carry a 20% risk of being infected with the hepatitis C virus (HCV; Rosenberg et al., 2001). Injection drug users have the highest incidence of HCV infection and are the fastest-growing population contracting new HCV infection. Alcoholics with liver disease compared with alcoholics without liver disease have a higher rate of HCV (Coelho-Little et al., 1995). Many clients with HIV also have hepatitis B and C. Clinicians are urged to discuss the importance of HCV testing with their clients who inject drugs or have a serious mental illness, alcoholism, and multiple sex partners.

Fatigue is the most common symptom in clients with chronic HCV (Crone et al., 2004). Depression and sleep problems have also been reported. Treatment for hepatitis C is available. Early treatment can prevent or slow liver damage. Alpha-interferons and ribavirin are the available treatments for hepatitis C. The side effects of these medications can include severe depression, suicidal tendencies, sleep problems, and fatigue.

HCV-infected clients with mental illness and substance use disorders can benefit from HCV treatments. Stabilizing their psychiatric problems, maintaining abstinence from substances, and optimizing their commitment to treatment makes them good candidates for treatment. Clinicians should advocate for their clients by collaborating with HCV treatment providers. Once they receive treatment, clients should be monitored closely for worsening of their psychiatric symptoms and risk of suicide.

Relapse Prevention and Progress Measurement

Chapter 18   *Reducing the Risk of Relapse*

(Corresponds to chapter 16 of the workbook)

Materials Needed

- Relapse Warning Signs Worksheet

- High-Risk Situations Worksheet

Objectives

- To introduce the client to the concepts of lapse and relapse in recovery from substance use disorders

- To help the client learn about warning signs that frequently precede relapse and develop strategies to manage them

- To help the client identify potential high-risk situations and strategies to manage them

Introduction

Any client who attempts to modify alcohol, tobacco, or drug use behavior faces the possibility of lapse or relapse (Carroll, 1996; Daley & Marlatt, 2005; Marlatt & Donovan, 2005). A *lapse* refers to the initial episode of use following a period of abstinence. A lapse may involve limited use of a substance (e.g., a few drinks, cigarettes, or hits on a joint) or excessive use (e.g., actually getting intoxicated or high). A lapse may be quickly stopped by the client or it may lead to a *relapse*, or continued use of a substance. How a client interprets and responds to a lapse plays a significant role in whether or not it leads to a relapse. For example, if a client feels guilty and despondent over drinking after months of sobriety and tells herself, "I'm a failure" or "I'm not capable of stopping my alcohol use," she is likely to continue drinking. On the other hand, if a client tells herself, "I made a mistake and had better cut things off before they get worse," her lapse is less likely to lead to a relapse. In the latter example, the lapse turns into a *prolapse*, in which the client quickly uses positive coping strategies and learns something from the mistake that will aid ongoing recovery.

The risk of lapse or relapse is highest in the first 3 months of recovery, during which time about two out of three relapses occur. Often, though not always, a return to substance use is one decision among many that are made over a period of hours, days, or even longer. Many clients, for example, state that their relapse built up gradually and that actual substance use was preceded by relapse warning signs.

Low motivation and poor participation in therapy or self-help programs can raise the risk of relapse, even for clients who recently completed a rehabilitation program. Other precipitants of relapse include psychiatric illness or an inability to cope with the challenges of recovery. Helping clients remain in therapy, identify early relapse warning signs, and identify high-risk situations are ways for the therapist to lower the client's risk of relapse.

Major Points and Issues for Discussion

The following are major points and issues for discussion:

1. The therapist discusses the difference between a lapse and a relapse and how the client's initial response to a lapse determines whether it leads to a relapse. What are the client's beliefs about relapse? Some clients believe they are invulnerable to relapse, believe they have learned their lesson so that relapse could never happen to them, or believe they don't need to make any changes in themselves or their lifestyle to aid their long-term recovery.

2. The therapist discusses the importance of identifying relapse warning signs. The earlier the client identifies potential or actual warning signs, the more able he or she will be to take action to

prevent a relapse. The client should develop a plan before experiencing warning signs.

3. The client needs to be educated about both obvious and subtle relapse warning signs, as well as about idiosyncratic warning signs. Idiosyncratic warning signs are those unique to each client in recovery. If the client has any previous experiences with relapse, these can be explored in detail to help him or her identify obvious and subtle warning signs. If the client is new to recovery, examples of these common warning signs preceding substance us relapse can be reviewed: (a) stopping or cutting down therapy sessions without making an agreement with the therapist that this is appropriate, (b) getting so busy that treatment-related activities are forgotten or given a low priority, (c) stopping or cutting down attendance at self-help meetings without discussing this decision with someone who knows about the client's recovery plan, (d) experiencing a significant increase in desires or thoughts of using and letting these build up, (e) stopping or decreasing other specific recovery behaviors (e.g., not completing a daily inventory, not participating in stress-reducing activities, not participating in pleasant activities), and (f) putting oneself in situations that are set-ups for relapse.

4. The client completes the Relapse Warning Signs Worksheet (Figure 18.1). On this worksheet, the client lists potential warning signs and identifies strategies for managing them, which are discussed with the therapist.

5. The therapist emphasizes the importance of anticipating and planning to cope with high-risk relapse situations as a way of better preparing for recovery. High-risk situations are those in which the client used alcohol, tobacco, or other drugs in the past, as well as any situation raising the client's vulnerability to using substances.

6. The client is educated about common categories of high-risk situations and relates to these on a personal level so he or she can identify personal high-risk situations. The most common high-risk situations include (a) negative or upsetting emotional states, (b) social pressures to engage in substance use, (c) interpersonal conflict, (d) internal thoughts of using or desire to "test" oneself,

Relapse Warning Signs Worksheet

Instructions: In the left column, list the attitudes, thoughts, and behaviors that are warning signs of potential relapse. In the right column, write strategies for coping with each of these situations.

Relapse warning signs	Coping strategies
Begin to miss crack and the action of getting high.	Remind myself that the action of getting high caused girlfriend to leave. Getting high usually led to trouble in my life. Keep busy to limit free time on my hands. Join the Y to swim and play ball regularly.
Want to blow off NA meetings.	Talk it over with other NAs and sponsor. Examine real reasons for wanting to blow off meetings. Remind myself of benefits of meetings. Review track list of clean time to see how meetings are associated with staying clean.
Focus on new women instead of the NA program's steps.	Avoid going out after meetings alone with any new woman I meet. Don't give out my phone number or ask for phone numbers of women. Do an honesty check and ask myself what the real reasons are for this behavior.
Start to forget to do my daily review at the end of each day.	Figure out why I'm slacking off my program. Do my review before I get too tired and fall asleep, because I use this as an excuse. Keep a reminder note on the bathroom mirror to prompt me to take 10 minutes for my daily review.

Figure 18.1

Example of a completed Relapse Warning Signs Worksheet.

High-Risk Situations Worksheet

Instructions: List three of your high-risk situations below. For each high-risk situation, list positive coping strategies.

High-risk situation 1	Coping strategies
I work too much and wear myself out.	Limiting long work days to no more than 2 each week. Take at least 1 full day off each week. Do something fun every single week. Take some time each day to relax and do whatever I want, including doing nothing. Tell myself I don't have to work all the time to prove I'm productive.

High-risk situation 2	Coping strategies
My boyfriend drinks a lot and likes us to go to bars and clubs, and we seem to argue a lot.	Reassess this relationship because he's not supporting my recovery; try to figure out why he'd want me to go, even though I'm trying to stay sober. In the meantime, don't go to bars or clubs, and suggest other social activities. Get to the bottom of why we're always at each other's throat, arguing and yelling. Stop my constant criticisms of him because this gets him going.

High-risk situation 3	Coping strategies
Feeling depressed about how my life is going.	Keep in mind that things are better since I got sober. Focus on one problem area at a time. Remember that I have a big say in how I feel, that I can take positive steps to change.

Figure 18.2

Example of a completed High-Risk Situations Worksheet.

and (e) strong cravings for alcohol, tobacco, or other drugs (Marlatt & Donovan, 2005). It is not the high-risk factor but the client's coping skills that usually determine whether substances are used following a period of recovery.

7. The client completes the High-Risk Situations Worksheet (Figure 18.2). Completing this worksheet will enable the client to begin identifying high-risk situations and positive coping skills to determine if there are specific deficits. For example, if a client identifies interpersonal disputes as a relapse risk and has a poor ability to negotiate differences with others, a deficit exists that raises his or her vulnerability to relapse, and this would be an appropriate target of therapy.

8. The therapist uses the information from the worksheet to help the client develop strategies for managing his or her high-risk situations. The focus is on helping the client develop specific skills to deal with the problems identified. For example, if a client identified "angry feelings" as a major relapse threat and typically dealt with anger by internalizing it, she would need help in learning how to express anger appropriately in interpersonal situations. She may also need to change her beliefs about anger to facilitate learning new behavioral skills.

9. A daily inventory is a way for the client to continuously monitor high-risk situations. The therapist encourages the client to take a few minutes at the end of each day to identify any current high-risk situations and develop plans to cope with them. For example, if an upcoming family visit during the holidays represents a high-risk situation for a client who is trying to abstain from alcohol, he could prepare to cope with the specific pressures he expects to face before making the trip. A "relapse roadmap" would help him chart his strategy ahead of time so that he will be better prepared to handle the situation. Waiting until he is actually with his family before planning relapse prevention might be too late.

10. A written journal is another way for the client to monitor and reflect on recovery issues and experiences. There are various ways of using journals with clients. One is to have the client purchase a

notebook (or use the computer) to regularly write about recovery. The client can choose what to write in the journal (e.g., reflections on the day). Or, the clinician can provide journal assignments (e.g., reflections on anger, forgiveness, or making amends). Another way is to use a structured written guide such as *Sobriety Journal: Your Plan for Recovery in Year One* (Daley, 2005), which provides easy-to-use checklists during the early months of recovery. A structured electronic journal is another way to help clients monitor and reflect upon their recovery (www.stayingsober.lifejournal.com).

Homework for Client

- Complete the Relapse Warning Signs Worksheet.

- Complete the High-Risk Situations Worksheet.

Chapter 19 *Relapse Management*

(Corresponds to chapter 17 of the workbook)

Materials Needed

- Lapse and Relapse Worksheet

- Relapse Chain Worksheet

Objectives

- To help the client identify strategies to interrupt an actual lapse or relapse

- To raise the client's awareness of his or her emotional and cognitive reactions to a lapse and how these reactions may lead to a relapse

- To complete a "relapse debriefing" to help the client learn from a lapse or relapse; this includes a review of the client's thoughts and feelings, as well as the circumstances, events, or decisions that led to the lapse or relapse

Introduction

Even if clients are working toward total abstinence, they should be prepared to handle setbacks, because many clients who are attempting to quit alcohol, tobacco, or other drugs will use substances again. Knowing how to interrupt a lapse or relapse can help clients minimize the damage associated with a return to substance use.

Lapses or relapses can be viewed as opportunities to learn from mistakes. Clients can use them to get back on track, change their recovery plan, or focus on learning new skills. As stated in the previous chapter, how a client responds to an initial lapse plays a significant role in whether the lapse leads to a relapse. Clients who lapse and then judge themselves harshly as failures or have strong feelings of demoralization are at risk to continue using substances. In addition to feeling like they let themselves down, clients may experience guilt and shame and feel that they let others down, including family, other friends in recovery, and even therapists.

Major Points and Issues for Discussion

The following are major points and issues for discussion:

1. The therapist discusses the importance of being able to interrupt a lapse or relapse in order to minimize the adverse effects on the client and his or her family. Usually, though not always, damage is minimized when the situation is controlled early. For example, physicians, other healthcare professionals, or athletes who are being monitored by employers or a state regulatory agency could suffer consequences for one positive drug test, regardless of how small a quantity of the drug is detected.

2. The therapist helps the client focus on strategies to catch setbacks as early as possible. Specific strategies can be rehearsed ahead of time so that the client feels more confident in his or her ability to use them. For example, a client may agree that a reasonable strategy to interrupt a lapse or relapse is to talk it over with a friend in a self-help program or with a therapist. However, the client may not be sure how to raise the issue or what to say, and may need guidance in how to disclose the experience. When the therapist initially orients the client to treatment, it helps to emphasize the importance of honesty in self-disclosing any episodes of use during treatment. If the client keeps secrets about lapses or relapses, this puts the therapist at a disadvantage. The process of therapy is more productive when the client self-discloses struggles and problems, including any episode of use.

3. If this is the client's first time in recovery, the therapist should ask him to imagine having a lapse, then describe his reactions to it. What could cause the lapse? What would the client feel after the initial episode of substance use? What would he think? What would happen next? What could the client do to stop the lapse from becoming a relapse?

Lapse and Relapse Worksheet

Instructions: Answer the following questions to help you figure out what led to your first drink, cigarette, or other drug use after having quit.

1. Describe the main reason you took the first drink, cigarette, or other drug.

   I smoked again because I wanted one real bad. It was a hard day at work.

2. Describe your inner thoughts and feelings that triggered your need or desire for the first drink, cigarette, or other drug.

   I felt anxious and tense, I thought I deserved something to relax me and calm me down after the day I had at work.

3. Describe any external circumstances that triggered your need or desire for the first drink, cigarette, or other drug.

   My husband started an argument with me over the budget. He said it was my fault we had so many bills. This made me mad.

4. Describe the first decision you made that started the lapse or relapse process.

   I decided to hide the budget from my husband for a few days even though I knew this would lead to an argument and problems down the road.

Figure 19.1

Examples of a completed Lapse and Relapse Worksheet.

4. If the client has experienced a lapse or relapse before, he completes the Lapse and Relapse Worksheet (Figure 19.1). This worksheet will help the client identify the main reasons for the lapse, including thoughts, feelings, circumstances, or events that triggered the substance use. The client with a history of multiple relapses should complete this worksheet for several recent relapses. Are there any patterns to the client's lapses or relapses in terms of warning signs, where and when they occur, how long they last, and their impact on the client's life?

5. The therapist reviews the concept of relapse as a process and states that actual substance use is the last link in a chain. Earlier links represent specific relapse warning signs or decisions that led the client away from recovery and toward relapse.

Lapse and Relapse Worksheet *continued*

Instructions: Answer the following questions to help you figure out what led to your first drink, cigarette, or other drug use after having quit.

1. Describe the main reason you took the first drink, cigarette, or other drug.

I went out on a date with this guy I really liked. He suggested a certain wine with our dinner so I didn't bother to tell him I was trying to stay off booze.

2. Describe your inner thoughts and feelings that triggered your need or desire for the first drink, cigarette, or other drug.

I felt excited to be with him and didn't want to disappoint him because he seemed to know so much about wine. I thought it seemed silly that I couldn't have a glass or two of wine with dinner.

3. Describe any external circumstances that triggered your need or desire for the first drink, cigarette, or other drug.

I wanted to get to know this man better and thought a few glasses of wine would make it easier to open up to him.

4. Describe the first decision you made that started the lapse or relapse process.

I decided to go out on a date with a man that I was pretty sure was a drinker.

Figure 19.1 *continued*

6. The client who has had a relapse completes the Relapse Chain Worksheet (Figure 19.2). In addition to helping identify warning signs that preceded a past relapse, this worksheet helps the client figure out how much time may have elapsed between early warning signs and actual substance use. In some instances, the process is quick; in other cases, early warning signs precede substance use by weeks or months.

7. The therapist discusses the actual and potential effects of a lapse or relapse. If the client has had lapses or relapse, he or she can describe the effects of the lapse or relapse on his or her life and significant relationships. Effects will vary from mild to severe. For example, we have had clients whose relapses to alcohol or other drug use have led to significant losses of relationships, jobs, housing stability, and psychiatric stability.

Instructions: Answer the following questions to help you figure out what led to your first drink, cigarette, or other drug use after having quit.

1. Describe the main reason you took the first drink, cigarette, or other drug.

I felt pressure to fit in with my friends who were drinking and using cocaine. I wanted to be one of the guys and not stick out because I wasn't getting high.

2. Describe your inner thoughts and feelings that triggered your need or desire for the first drink, cigarette, or other drug.

I felt awkward, plus it was boring to watch the guys have a good time getting high. I thought what the hell, I'll just have a few beers. Don't use cocaine and I'll be cool.

3. Describe any external circumstances that triggered your need or desire for the first drink, cigarette, or other drug.

Once I drank a few beers, it was only a matter of time until I snorted some coke. The high from the beer wasn't good enough and I had to have cocaine. Soon, I was using regularly.

4. Describe the first decision you made that started the lapse or relapse process.

I decided that I could hang out with the guys and not use cocaine; that as long as I watched myself, I would be OK.

Figure 19.1 *continued*

8. Because it isn't unusual for family members or significant others to react negatively to a client's substance use, have the client discuss his or her experiences with others' reactions. If the client has not had a lapse or relapse, he or she can think of potential reactions of family or significant others. Unfortunately, in some instances, clients may pay a steep price for a lapse or relapse. For example, a client's partner may end the relationship if the client uses drugs following a period of recovery.

Homework for Client

▪ Complete the Lapse and Relapse Worksheet.

▪ Complete the Relapse Chain Worksheet.

Relapse Chain Worksheet

Instructions: The last link in the relapse chain represents your use of alcohol, tobacco, or other drugs. Each preceding link represents a specific relapse warning sign. Identify as many warning signs as you can. Then state how much time elapsed between the earliest warning sign and the first time you used a substance again. Also, state how you felt about using substances again, and how your family (or other significant people in your life) felt.

Found a couple of joints in my drawer when looking for a sweater.

Thought a few hits would be nice, but didn't use any, put joint back in drawer.

Didn't make any weekend plans.

At work, thought about what a drag the weekend had been.

Called Arlene who invited me to a party on Saturday.

Told myself I was ready for a party, that if I couldn't go and not get high, I'd never beat this thing.

Went to her party

Invited Arlene over to my house the next week for lunch.

She asked me if I'd mind if she smoked a joint, I said go ahead.

After she lit up, I took a few hits and later went out for a few drinks.

Time elapsed from early warning signs to actual use: _3 weeks_

How I felt about using again: _Excited at first, then guilty and shameful._

How my family or significant others felt: _Upset, disappointed, and angry._

Figure 19.2

Example of a completed Relapse Chain Worksheet.

Chapter 20 | *Strategies for Balanced Living*

(Corresponds to chapter 18 of the workbook)

Materials Needed

- Teeter-Totter Balance Test

- Lifestyle Balance Worksheet

- Pleasant Activities Worksheet

Objectives

- To help the client evaluate the major dimensions of life to determine which areas are out of balance and how to work toward better balance

- To teach the client how to use a daily inventory to catch problems that could lead to imbalance in life

- To teach the client how to build structure and pleasant activities into daily life

Introduction

Achieving balance in life can protect the client from relapse. The more balanced and satisfying a client's life is, the less the client needs to use substances to feel good, escape, gain excitement, or cope with problems. *Balance* refers to the client's ability to meet his or her responsibilities or obligations and to take care of his or her unique personal needs and wants. A healthy lifestyle involves the ability to reasonably balance various aspects of life: physical, emotional, intellectual, creative, family, interpersonal, spiritual, work or school, and financial. Balanced living also contributes to personal growth and happiness.

Because life is full of demands and responsibilities, it isn't unusual for some areas of life to become unbalanced from time to time. The important issue for the client is living with temporary periods of imbalance when they are unavoidable or necessary and working toward better balance when possible.

Major Points and Issues for Discussion

The following are major points and issues for discussion:

1. The therapist discusses the concept of balance in life from two perspectives: (a) the need for balance between obligations and wants and (b) the need for balance and satisfaction among the major dimensions of life (work, family, relationships, etc.).

2. The client completes the Teeter-Totter Balance Test (Figure 20.1). This exercise provides a global overview of the client's obligations versus his or her needs.

3. Balanced living can help raise the client's level of satisfaction with life and reduce the risk of relapse. If imbalance is too great and the client is overwhelmed by too many obligations or pressures, the temptation to escape or experience pleasure through substance use may increase. To address this issue, the client should look at all areas of life to determine which ones are out of balance and need attention. Once identified, areas of imbalance can be targeted for change.

4. The client completes the Lifestyle Balance Worksheet (Figure 20.2). This worksheet poses a number of questions in nine major areas of life functioning. The client's answers to these questions will help determine which of the following areas are out of balance and need to be worked on: physical, mental or emotional, intellectual, creative or artistic, family, personal relationships, spiritual, work or school, and financial.

5. Some periods of imbalance are inevitable due to the demands of living or particular circumstances. For example, a client who is

Teeter-Totter Balance Test

Wants List	Shoulds List
Take fun breaks at work	Go to work
Buy myself a treat	Pay bills
Go to a movie after chores	Do chores
Plan a vacation	Take care of relatives

Figure 20.1

Example of a completed Teeter-Totter Balance Test.

both working full-time and attending school will need to devote sufficient time to studying in order to meet her goals. This may mean that other areas, such as social relationships or creative and artistic endeavors, are put on hold or given less time and attention. A client who is a new mother is likely to have much less time to pursue personal interests than she would like due to the demands of child-rearing. The challenge is for the client not to ignore areas of life that are important to her well-being.

6. The therapist helps the client prioritize out-of-balance areas that need to be changed. The therapist and client work collaboratively to develop strategies for addressing areas to change.

7. Using a daily inventory or review is one way the client can catch problems before they cause imbalance in life (see Chapter 18 in the Workbook). A daily inventory can help the client monitor progress on a daily basis.

8. The client who needs to build more structure into life completes the Weekly Schedule Worksheet (see Chapter 18 in the Workbook). This is another way to identify and address the issue of lifestyle balance. For example, a client may be spending a disproportionate amount of time at work-related activities at the expense of impor-

Lifestyle Balance Worksheet

Instructions: Answer the following questions to help you determine how balanced your life is currently. Then review your answers. Identify two out-of-balance areas that you want to change. Write a plan for change in each area.

1. Physical:

Are you in good health?	✓ Yes	___ No
Do you exercise regularly?	___ Yes	✓ No
Do you follow a reasonable diet?	✓ Yes	___ No
Do you take good care of your appearance?	✓ Yes	___ No
Do you get sufficient rest and sleep?	✓ Yes	___ No
Do you get regular medical and dental checkups?	✓ Yes	___ No
Do you have strategies to handle cravings to use substances?	✓ Yes	___ No

2. Mental/emotional:

Are you experiencing excessive stress?	___ Yes	✓ No
Do you worry too much?	___ Yes	✓ No
Do you have strategies to reduce mental stress?	✓ Yes	___ No
Are you able to express your feelings to others?	___ Yes	✓ No
Do you suffer from serious depression or anxiety?	___ Yes	✓ No

3. Intellectual:

Are you able to satisfy your intellectual needs?	✓ Yes	___ No
Do you have enough interests to satisfy your intellectual curiosity?	✓ Yes	___ No

4. Creative/artistic:

Do you regularly participate in creative or artistic endeavors?	___ Yes	✓ No
Do you have talents or abilities that you think are not being used as much as you would like?	✓ Yes	___ No

5. Family:

Are you generally satisfied with your family relationships?	✓ Yes	___ No
Do you spend enough time with your family (especially your children, if you have any)?	___ Yes	✓ No
Can you rely on your family for help and support?	✓ Yes	___ No

6. Personal relationships:

Are you generally satisfied with the quantity and quality of your personal relationships?	✓ Yes	___ No
Do you have friends you can depend on for help and support?	✓ Yes	___ No
Are you able to express your ideas, needs, and feelings to others?	✓ Yes	___ No
Are there any specific relationships in which you have serious problems?	___ Yes	✓ No

Figure 20.2

Example of a completed Lifestyle Balance Worksheet.

7. Spiritual:

Is there enough love in your life?	✓ Yes	___ No
Do you pay enough attention to your "inner" spiritual life?	✓ Yes	___ No
Do you feel a sense of inner peace?	___ Yes	✓ No

8. Work or school

Are you usually satisfied with your work or school situation?	___ Yes	✓ No
Do you spend too much time or effort working?	✓ Yes	___ No
Do you spend too little time or effort working?	___ Yes	✓ No

9. Financial:

Do you have sufficient income to meet your expenses?	✓ Yes	___ No
Are you having any serious financial problems (e.g., too much debt, no savings, etc.)?	___ Yes	✓ No
Do you handle your money responsibilities with an eye to the future?	✓ Yes	___ No
Does money play too big a role in your life?	___ Yes	✓ No

Out-of-balance area:

I don't spend enough time with my family.

My change plan:

Have dinner with my family at least 3 evenings during the week.

Plan family activities at least once each weekend.

Take my wife out alone at least once a month.

Spend at least 1 hour each week alone with each of my kids.

Plan a weekend trip with my family.

Out-of-balance area:

I spend too much time working.

My change plan:

Work late only 2 days per week.

Carefully keep track of how much time I work.

Delegate more work to employees I supervise.

Limit work I do at home on weekends to one block of time on Saturday.

Get back to playing tennis every week and avoid being too busy at work as an excuse for

why I can't play.

Figure 20.2 *continued*

Pleasant Activities Worksheet

Instructions: List current activities that you consider to be a pleasant part of your life. Then, think of several new activities to try. These should be activities in which there is no or minimal pressure to use alcohol or other drugs.

Current pleasant activities

Jogging

Going to new movies

Watching old movies

Visiting friends

Visiting my sister and her family

Reading novels

Playing with my children

Coffee in the morning with my husband

Reading the paper after dinner

Watching the news before bedtime

Taking hot baths

New pleasant activities

Learn how to ski

Go to a jazz concert with my husband

Go swimming with my children

Learn how to use the Internet on the computer

Read biographies of people I admire

Figure 20.3

Example of a completed Pleasant Activities Worksheet.

tant relationships or leisure activities. Although structure is often helpful, it is also important to have some unstructured time.

9. One way for the client to work toward balance between obligations and needs is to complete the Pleasant Activities Worksheet (Figure 20.3). On this worksheet the client lists current activities that he or she enjoys, as well as new, pleasant activities to try. This

exercise can help the client identify and plan new activities that are fun or enjoyable or add to better balance in life. As simple as this sounds, however, it isn't unusual for clients to struggle in pursuing a new activity. Clients create many excuses for why a new activity cannot be pursued. The therapist can help the client anticipate some of these roadblocks and better prepare him or her for change.

Homework for Client

- Complete the Teeter-Totter Balance Test.
- Complete the Lifestyle Balance Worksheet.
- Take a few minutes at the end of each day to complete a daily inventory.
- Complete the Weekly Schedule Worksheet to help plan your week.
- Complete the Pleasant Activities Worksheet.

Chapter 21 | *Measuring Progress*

(Corresponds to chapter 19 of the workbook)

Objectives

- To help the client evaluate progress against goals identified in his or her change plan

- To help the client be realistic about ways in which to measure progress

- To help the client modify "all or none" beliefs about progress in order to appreciate small changes

Introduction

Progress in recovery is measured according to the client's goals. It is helpful for the client to periodically review his or her progress and check it against his or her goals; this helps the client to see if he or she is making progress and to identify new goals and recovery strategies. Clients sometimes minimize their progress, especially when they have temporary setbacks. Viewing progress realistically helps improve the client's motivation to continue working toward recovery and reinforces positive changes, no matter how small.

There are many ways to measure progress. Although the ideal goal is total abstinence from alcohol or other drugs, any movement toward this goal can be viewed as progress. For example, a client who comes to treatment with very little interest in changing substance use behavior, then begins to rethink this position and examine his substance use, is making progress. Another client who was a daily user is abstinent for several weeks or months. Even though she has a relapse, this client is still moving in the right direction and making progress.

In some instances, progress is large and obvious. In other instances, it has to be measured in small changes. Progress can be measured in terms of cessation or reduction of substance use as well as improvement in other areas of life.

Major Points and Issues for Discussion

The following are major points and issues for discussion:

1. The therapist and client review the client's progress to date. Progress is discussed in relation to the treatment goals outlined in the original change plan. The discussion should be balanced between positive steps made to date and changes that the client still wants to make. The client should review progress often during the initial weeks or months of recovery (e.g., weekly at first).

2. If the client is unable to make any progress with the current plan, other treatment options are discussed. For example, if a client did not make much headway on his alcohol problem with weekly or biweekly therapy sessions, the frequency of sessions could be increased, or a more intensive level of treatment, such as an intensive outpatient program, could be considered. Adding treatment to the existing plan (e.g., taking ReVia, participating in a therapy group in addition to individual sessions) could also be considered. If the client's treatment will be terminated, the therapist should review the client's plan for continued, post-treatment change.

3. Although each client needs to measure progress against his or her personal goals, any of the following milestones indicates that progress is being made: (a) the client is moving from one stage of the change process to another (e.g., from contemplation to preparation, from preparation to action), (b) the client is able to maintain abstinence from alcohol or other drugs, (c) the client reduces the amount and frequency of substance use, (d) the client experiences a decrease in the harmful effects of substance use, (e) the client's health or life has improved in one or more ways (e.g., physical health, spirituality, relationships), (f) the client experiences a decrease in obsession and craving to use substances, (g) the client feels more hopeful or confident about his or her ability to make

positive changes and handle problems, (h) the client is more aware of high-risk situations, is willing to discuss them, and has a plan to cope with them, (i) the client is willing to discuss setbacks in detail in order to learn from them, (j) the client cuts off a lapse or relapse more quickly than in the past, (k) the client is able to use a variety of strategies or skills to cope with problems and challenges in recovery, or (l) the client is willing to alter his or her change plan if the current approach is not working effectively. The client can elicit feedback from others about his or her progress. For example, sponsors or friends in recovery who know the client well or family members who are aware of the client's recovery process can point out ways in which he or she is making progress.

4. The therapist should help clients avoid the common trap of judging progress in absolute, "all or none" terms. Otherwise, unless clients make substantial changes, they may feel demoralized, give up, or judge themselves to be incapable of change. The therapist should discuss ways in which clients can reward themselves for positive changes made, no matter how small. Clients should reward themselves for efforts to change as well as actual changes. Many people work hard, only to stumble on the way to change. However, putting forth a good effort can be a positive experience, as long as the effort is not overlooked and taken for granted. Trying to change and failing is better than not trying to change at all.

Case Examples

Mike (Alcohol)

Mike is a 38-year-old, self-employed, married father of two children who has been in three rehabilitation programs and two outpatient programs for alcoholism during the past 7 years. He has been alcohol-free for over 5 months, the longest he's ever been sober. Mike attends AA meetings regularly and talks openly about his occasional desires to drink alcohol. He has not missed any outpatient therapy sessions in the past 5 months, a big improvement compared to the past, when he seldom kept his appointments and dropped out of treatment early only to re-

lapse again. Whereas his marriage had been on the brink of falling apart, he and his wife are getting along well now. Mike has taken an active role with his children too. Clearly, he's made many strides in his recovery to date. ■

Lana (Marijuana)

■ *Lana is a 26-year-old secretary with a 5-year history of marijuana abuse. At her worst, she was smoking several joints a day. Lana is frustrated because she feels her life hasn't gotten any better since she quit smoking marijuana 8 months ago. However, when she and her therapist closely examined her life, Lana discovered that she is better off in several ways now that she's drug-free: she has not missed work at all since stopping drugs, whereas before she routinely used all of her sick leave early in the year; she has saved several hundred dollars each month, compared to previously saving nothing; she's planning to go back to night school because she wants to get a better-paying job and establish a different career; and her overall mood is slightly better than when she smoked marijuana regularly.* ■

Lindsey (Tobacco)

■ *Lindsey is a 51-year-old millwright with a lifelong pattern of smoking up to three packs of cigarettes a day. He first quit smoking over a year ago at the advice of his family doctor. Lindsey has had two lapses and one relapse since this time, lasting from 1 day to 4 weeks. During the 4-week relapse, he smoked daily, but seldom more than a pack a day—a big improvement over the past. He realized from these experiences that he cannot safely smoke a limited number of cigarettes. Lindsey also realized that he has more stamina when he doesn't smoke and that his wife is more affectionate when he doesn't reek of cigarettes.* ■

Homework for Client

■ Complete the Putting It All Together Worksheet.

Appendix *Helpful Resources*

There are many resources on substance use disorders, treatment, and recovery. These include informational resources for clinicians and individuals in recovery (books, treatment manuals, recovery guides, workbooks, audiotapes, and videotapes), as well as self-help programs such as AA, NA, and DRA. Treatment manuals and books for professionals are available from CSAT, NIAAA, NIDA, Hazelden, and Oxford University Press.

In addition to the websites below, resources can be accessed on the Internet through bookstores, publishers of recovery literature, or by conducting a search of key terms or words such as addiction; alcohol abuse, alcohol addiction, alcohol dependence, or alcoholism; drug abuse, drug addiction, or drug dependency; families and addiction; recovery from addiction; or the name of a specific substance, person, or organization associated with treatment of addiction or recovery.

Alcoholics Anonymous	www.aa.org
Al-Anon Family Groups	www.al-anon.org
Center for Substance Abuse Treatment (CSAT)	www.csat.samhsa.gov
Dennis C. Daley, PhD	www.drdenniscdaley.com
Dual Recovery Anonymous (DRA)	www.dualrecovery.org
Hazelden Educational Materials	www.hazelden.org
Life Journal	www.stayingsober.lifejournal.com
Narcotics Anonymous	www.na.org

Nar-Anon Family Groups	www.naranon.org
National Clearinghouse for Alcohol & Drug Information	www.health.org
National Institute on Alcohol Abuse and Alcoholism (NIAAA)	www.niaaa.nih.gov
National Institute on Drug Abuse (NIDA)	www.nida.nih.gov
National Institute of Mental Health	www.nimh.nih.gov
Treatments *That Work*™ series companion web site	www.oup.com/us/ttw

References and Suggested Readings

Alcoholics Anonymous ("Big Book," 4th ed.) (2001). New York: AA World Services, Inc.

Allen, J.P., Litten, R.Z., & Fertig, J.B. (1997). A review of research on the alcohol use disorders identification test (AUDIT). *Alcoholism: Clinical and Experimental Research, 21*(4), 613–619.

American Psychiatric Association. (2000a). *Diagnostic and Statistical Manual of Mental Disorders (DSM-IV-TR)*, 5th ed. Washington, DC: APA.

American Psychiatric Association. (2000b). *Handbook of Psychiatric Measures.* Washington, DC: APA.

American Psychiatric Association. (2004). *Practice Guidelines for the Treatment of Psychiatric Disorders.* Washington, DC: APA.

Andreasen, N.C. (2001). *Brave New Brain: Conquering Mental Illness in the Era of the Genome.* New York: Oxford University Press.

Antony, M.M., Barlow, D.H., & Craske, M.G. (1997). *Mastery of Your Specific Phobia: Therapist Guide.* San Antonio, TX: Psychological Corporation.

Antony, M.M., & Swinson, R.P. (2000). *Phobic Disorders and Panic Disorders in Adults: A Guide to Assessment and Treatment.* Washington, DC: American Psychological Association.

Baer, J.S., Kivlahan, D.R., Blume, A.W., Mc Knight, P., & Marlatt, G.A. (2001). Brief intervention for heavy drinking college students: 4-year follow-up and natural history. *American Journal of Public Health*, 91, 1310–1316.

Basco, M.R., & Rush, A.J. (1996). *Cognitive-Behavioral Therapy for Bipolar Disorder.* New York: Guilford Press.

Beck, A.T. (1976). *Cognitive Therapy of the Emotional Disorders.* New York: International Universities Press.

Beck, A.T., Freeman, A., Davis, D.D., & Associates (2004). *Cognitive Therapy of Personality Disorders.* New York: Guilford.

Beck, A.T., Wright, F.D., Newman, C.F., & Liese, B.S. (1993). *Cognitive Therapy of Substance Abuse.* New York: Guilford.

Bellack, A.S., & DiClemente, C.G. (1999). Treating substance abuse among patients with schizophrenia. *Psychiatric Services, 50,* 75–80.

Bellack, A.S., Mueser, K.T., Gingerich, S., & Agresta, J. (2004). *Social Skills Training for Schizophrenia,* 2nd ed. New York: Guilford Press.

Berrettini, W.H., & Lerman, C.E. (2005). Pharmacotherapy and pharma-cogenetics of nicotine dependence. *American Journal of Psychiatry, 162*(8), 1441–1451.

Bien, T.H., Miller, W.R., & Tonigan, J.S. (1993). Brief interventions for alcohol problems: a review. *Addiction, 88,* 315–336.

Bongar, B. (2002). *The Suicidal Patient: Clinical and Legal Standards of Care,* 2nd ed. Washington, DC: American Psychological Association.

Bongar, B., Berman, A.L., Maris, R.W., Silverman, J.M., Harris, E.A., & Packman, W.L. (Eds.). (1998). *Risk Management with Suicidal Patients.* New York: Guilford Press.

Brady, K.T., & Sinha, R. (2005). Co-occurring mental and substance use disorders: The neurobiological effects of chronic stress. *American Journal of Psychiatry, 162*(8), 1483–1493.

Brown, P.J., Muellar, T., & Stout, R.L. (1999). Substance use disorder and posttraumatic stress disorder comorbidity: Addiction and psychiatric treatment rates. *Psychology of Addictive Behaviors, 13*(2), 115–122.

Burns, D. (1999). *Feeling Good: The New Mood Therapy.* New York: Avon Books.

Carroll, K.M. (1996). Relapse prevention as a psychosocial treatment: a review of controlled clinical trials. *Experimental and Clinical Psychopharmacology, 4,* 46–54.

Carroll, K.M., & Onken, L.S. (2005). Behavioral therapies for drug abuse. *American Journal of Psychiatry, 162*(8), 1452–1460.

Center for Mental Health Services (CMHS). (1998). *Co-occurring Psychiatric and Substance Disorders in Managed Care Systems: Standards of Care, Practice Guidelines, Workforce Competencies, and Training Curricula.* Rockville, MD: CMHS.

Center for Substance Abuse Treatment. (1994). *Simple Screening Instruments for Outreach for Alcohol and Other Drug Abuse and Infectious Disease.* TIP 11. Rockville, MD: U.S. Department of Health and Human Services.

Center for Substance Abuse Treatment. (1999a). *Brief Interventions and Brief Therapists for Substance Abuse.* TIP 34. Rockville, MD: U.S. Department of Health and Human Services.

Center for Substance Abuse Treatment. (1999b). *Enhancing Motivation to Change in Substance Abuse Treatment.* TIP 35. Rockville, MD: U.S. Department of Health and Human Services.

Center for Substance Abuse Treatment. (1999c). *Treatment Succeeds in Fighting Crime.* Rockville, MD: CSAT.

Center for Substance Abuse Treatment. (2000a). *Substance Abuse Treatment: Reduces Family Dysfunction, Improves Productivity.* Rockville, MD: CSAT.

Center for Substance Abuse Treatment. (2000b). *Treatment Cuts Medical Costs.* Rockville, MD: CSAT.

Center for Substance Abuse Treatment. (2002). *Assessment and Treatment of Patients with Coexisting Mental Illness and Other Drug Abuse.* DHHS Pub. No. (SMA) 02–3682. Rockville, MD: U.S. Department of Health and Human Services.

Center for Substance Abuse Treatment. (2004a). *Clinical Guidelines for the Use of Buprenorphine in the Treatment of Opioid Addiction.* TIP 40. Rockville, MD: U.S. Department of Health and Human Services.

Center for Substance Abuse Treatment. (2004b). *Substance Abuse Treatment and Family Therapy.* TIP 39. Rockville, MD: U.S. Department of Health and Human Services

Center for Substance Abuse Treatment. (2005a). *Medication Assistant Treatment for Opioid Addiction in Opioid Treatment Programs.* TIP 43. Rockville, MD: U.S. Department of Health and Human Services.

Center for Substance Abuse Treatment. (2005b). *Substance Abuse Treatment: Group Therapy.* TIP 41. Rockville, MD: U.S. Department of Health and Human Services.

Center for Substance Abuse Treatment. (2005c). *Substance Abuse Treatment for Persons with Co-Occurring Disorders.* TIP 42. Rockville, MD: U.S. Department of Health and Human Services.

Clark, R.E. (2001). Family support and substance use outcomes for persons with mental illness and substance use disorders. *Schizophrenia Bulletin, 27*(1), 93–101.

Cloninger, C.R. (1987). Neurogenetic adaptive mechanisms in alcoholism. *Science,* 410–416.

Cloninger, C.R. (2005). Genetics of substance abuse. In M. Galanter & H.D. Kleber (Eds.), *Textbook of Substance Abuse Treatment,* 3rd ed. Washington, DC: American Psychiatric Publishing, Inc., pp. 73–80.

Cloninger, C.R., & Svrakic, D.M. (2000). Personality disorders. In B.J. Sadock & V.A. Sadock (Eds.), *Comprehensive Textbook of Psychiatry,* 7th ed. Baltimore, MD: Lippincott Williams & Wilkins, pp. 1723–1764.

Connors, G.J., Donovan, D.M., & DiClemente, C.C. (2001). *Substance Abuse Treatment and the Stages of Change.* New York: Guilford Press.

Cornelius, J.R., Salloum, I.M., Day, N.L., Thase, M.E., & Mann, J.J. (1996). Patterns of suicidality and alcohol use in alcoholics with major depression. *Alcoholism: Clinical and Experimental Research, 20,* 1451–1455.

Cornelius, J.R., Salloum, I.M., Ehler, J.G., et al. (1997). Fluoxetine in depressed alcoholics. A double-blind, placebo-controlled trial. *Archives of General Psychiatry, 54*(8), 700–705.

Crits-Christoph, P., Siqueland, L., Blaine J., et al. (1999). Psychosocial treatments for cocaine dependence: National Institute on Drug Abuse collaborative cocaine treatment study. *Archives of General Psychiatry, 56,* 493–502.

Crone, C.C., Gabriel, G.M., & Wise, T.N. (2004). Managing the neuropsychiatric side effects of interferon-based therapy for hepatitis C. *Cleveland Clinic Journal of Medicine, 71* (Suppl.): S27–S32.

Daley, D.C. (2003a). *Dual Diagnosis Workbook: Recovery Strategies for Substance Use and Mental Health Disorders,* 3rd ed. Independence, MO: Independence Press.

Daley, D.C. (2003b). *Preventing Relapse,* 2nd ed. Center City, MN: Hazelden.

Daley, D.C. (2004a). *Relapse Prevention Workbook,* 4th ed. Apollo, PA: Daley Publications.

Daley, D.C. (2004b). *Surviving Addiction Workbook,* 3rd ed. Apollo, PA: Daley Publications.

Daley, D.C. (2005). *Sobriety Journal: Your Plan for Recovery in Year 01.* Apollo, PA: Daley Publications.

Daley, D.C. (2006). *Mood Disorders and Addiction: A Guide for Clients, Families and Providers.* New York: Oxford University Press.

Daley, D.C., & Douaihy, A. (2005). *Managing Emotions: Recovery from Mental Health or Substance Use Disorders.* Apollo, PA: Daley Publications.

Daley, D.C., & Folit, R. (2006). *LifeJournal for Sobriety and Relapse Prevention.* www.stayingsober.lifejournal.com.

Daley, D.C., & Haskett, R. (2003). *Understanding Bipolar Disorder and Addiction,* 2nd ed. Center City, MN: Hazelden.

Daley, D.C., & Marlatt, G.A. (2005). Relapse prevention. In J.H. Lowinson, P. Ruiz, R.B. Millman, & J.G. Langrod (Eds.), *Substance Abuse: A Comprehensive Textbook,* 4th ed. Philadelphia: Lippincott Williams & Wilkins, pp. 772–785.

Daley, D.C., Marlatt, G.A., & Spotts, C. (2003a). Group therapies. In A.W. Graham, T.K. Schultz, M.F. Mayo-Smith, R.K. Ries, & B.K. Wilford (Eds.), *Principles of Addiction Medicine,* 3rd ed. Chevy Chase, MD: American Society of Addiction Medicine, pp. 839–850.

Daley, D.C., Marlatt, G.A., & Spotts, C. (2003b). Relapse prevention: clinical models and intervention strategies. In A.W. Graham, T.K. Schultz, M.F. Mayo-Smith, R.K. Ries, & B.K. Wilford (Eds.), *Principles of*

Addiction Medicine, 3rd ed. Chevy Chase, MD: American Society of Addiction Medicine, pp. 467–486.

Daley, D.C., Mercer, D., & Carpenter, G. (1998). *Group Drug Counseling Manual*. Holmes Beach, FL: Learning Publications, Inc.

Daley, D.C., & Miller, J. (2001). *Addiction in Your Family: Helping Yourself and Your Loved Ones*. Holmes Beach, FL: Learning Publications.

Daley, D.C., & Montrose, K. (2003). *Understanding Schizophrenia and Addiction*, 2nd ed. Center City, MN: Hazelden.

Daley, D.C., & Moss, H.B. (2002). *Dual Disorders: Counseling Clients with Chemical Dependency and Mental Illness*, 3rd ed. Center City, MN: Hazelden.

Daley, D.C., & Salloum, I.M. (Eds.). (2001). *A Clinician's Guide to Mental Illness*. New York: McGraw-Hill.

Daley, D.C., & Salloum, I.M. (2003). *Understanding Major Anxiety Disorders and Addiction*, 2nd ed. Center City, MN: Hazelden.

Daley, D.C., Salloum, I.M., & Thase, M.E. (2000). Improving treatment adherence among patients with comorbid psychiatric and substance use disorders. In D.F. O'Connell (Ed.), *Managing the Dually Diagnosed Patient: Current Issues and Clinical Approaches*. New York: Haworth Press, pp. 47–72.

Daley, D.C., Salloum, I.M., & Thase, M.E., (2003). Integrated treatment using a recovery oriented approach. In J.J. Westermeyer, R.D. Weiss & D.M. Ziedonis (Eds.), *Integrated Treatment for Mood and Substance Use Disorders*. Baltimore: Johns Hopkins University Press, pp. 68–89.

Daley, D.C., Salloum, I.M., Zuckoff, A., Kirisci, L., & Thase, M. (1998). Increasing treatment compliance among outpatients with depression and cocaine dependence. Results of a pilot study. *American Journal of Psychiatry, 155,* 1611–1613.

Daley, D.C., & Sinberg-Spear, J. (2003). *A Family Guide to Coping with Dual Disorders,* 3rd ed. Center City, MN: Hazelden.

Daley, D.C., & Thase, M.E. (2003). *Understanding Depression and Addiction,* 2nd ed. Center City, MN: Hazelden.

Daley, D.C., & Thase, M.E. (2004). *Dual Disorders Recovery Counseling: Integrated Treatment for Substance Use and Mental Health Disorders,* 3rd ed. Independence, MO: Independence Press.

Daley, D.C., & Zuckoff, A. (1999). *Improving Treatment Compliance: Counseling and System Strategies for Substance Use and Dual Disorders*. Center City, MN: Hazelden.

DeLeon, G. (2000). *The Therapeutic Community: Theory, Model and Method.* New York: Springer Publishing Co.

DiClemente, C.C. (2003). *Addiction and Change: How Addictions Develop and Addicted People Recover.* New York: Guilford Press

Donovan, D.M., & Marlatt, G.A. (Eds.). (2005). *Assessment of Addictive Behaviors,* 2nd ed. New York: Guilford Press.

Douaihy, A.B., Jou, R.J., Gorske, T., & Salloum, I.M. (2003). Triple diagnosis: Dual diagnosis and HIV disease, Part 1. *The Aids Reader, 13*(8): 375–382.

Drake, R.E., Mercer-McFadden, C., Mueser, K.T., McHugho, G., & Bond, G. (1998). A review of integrated mental health and substance abuse treatment for patients with dual disorders. *Schizophrenia Bulletin, 24,* 589–608.

Drake, R.E., & Mueser, K.T. (2000). Psychosocial approaches to dual diagnosis. *Schizophrenia Bulletin, 26*(1), 105–118.

Dual Disorders Recovery Book, The. (1993). Center City, MN: Hazelden.

Emrick, C.D., & Tonigan, J.S. (2004). Alcoholics Anonymous and other 12-step groups. In M. Galanter & H. Kleber (Eds.), *Textbook of Substance Abuse Treatment,* 3rd ed. Washington, DC: American Psychiatric Publishing Inc., pp. 433–444.

Fink, M. (1999). *Electroshock: Restoring the Mind.* New York: Oxford University Press.

First, M. B., Spitzer, R. L., Gibbon, M., & Williams, J. B. (1994). *Structured Clinical Interview for DSM-IV, Axis I Disorders.* New York: New York State Psychiatric Institute.

Foa, E.B., Keane, T.M., & Friedman, M.J. (Eds.). (2000). *Effective Treatments of PTSD.* New York: Guilford.

Frank, E. (2005). *Treating Bipolar Disorder: A Clinician's Guide to Interpersonal and Social Rhythm Therapy.* New York: Guilford Press.

Fromme, K., Marlatt, G. A., Baer, J. S., & Kivlahan, D.R. (1994). The alcohol skills training program: a group intervention for young adult drinkers. *Journal of Substance Abuse Treatment, 11*(2), 143–154.

Fundala, P.J., & O'Brien, C.P. (2005). Buprenorphine for the treatment of opioid dependence. In J.H. Lowinson, P. Ruiz, R.B. Millman, & J.G. Langrod (Eds.), *Substance Abuse: A Comprehensive Textbook,* 4th ed. Philadelphia: Lippincott Williams & Wilkins, pp.634–640.

Galanter, M., & Kleber, H. (Eds.). (2004). *Textbook of Substance Abuse Treatment,* 3rd ed. Washington, DC: American Psychiatric Publishing Inc.

Garbutt, J.C., West, S.L., Carey, T.S., Lohr, K.N., & Crews, F.T. (1999). Pharmacological treatment of alcohol dependence: a review of the evidence. *Journal of the American Medical Association, 281*(14), 1318–1325.

Gardner, E.L. (2005). Brain reward mechanisms. In J.H. Lowinson, P. Ruiz, R.B. Millman, & J.G. Langrod (Eds.), *Substance Abuse: A Comprehen-*

sive Textbook, 4th ed. Philadelphia: Lippincott Williams & Wilkins, pp. 48–96.

Gastfriend, D.R., & Perard, S. (2004). Patient placement criteria. In M. Galanter & H, Kleber (Eds.), *Textbook of Substance Abuse Treatment,* 3rd ed. Washington, DC: American Psychiatric Publishing Inc., pp. 121–128.

Graham, A.W., Schultz, T.K., & Wilford, B.B. (Eds.). (2003). *Principles of Addiction Medicine,* 3rd ed. Chevy Chase, MD: American Society of Addiction Medicine.

Gunderson, J.G., & Gabbard, G.O. (Eds.). (2000). *Psychotherapy for Personality Disorders.* Washington, DC: American Psychiatric Press.

Hawkins, J.D., Arthur, M.W., & Olson, J.J. (1997). Community interventions to reduce risks and enhance protection against antisocial behavior. In D.M. Stoff, J. Breiling, & J.D. Maser (Eds.), *Handbook of Antisocial Behavior.* New York: John Wiley and Sons, pp. 365–374.

Hazelden Foundation (Dec. 2004). *Research Update.* Center City, MN.

Hester, R.K., & Miller, W.R. (Eds.). (1995). *Handbook of Alcoholism Treatment Approaches: Effective Alternatives,* 2nd ed. Boston: Allyn and Bacon.

Higgins, S.T., & Hil, S.H. (2004). Principles of learning on the study and treatment of substance abuse. In M. Galanter & H. Kleber (Eds.), *Textbook of Substance Abuse Treatment,* 3rd ed. Washington, DC: American Psychiatric Publishing Inc., pp. 81–88.

Higgins, S.T., & Silverman, K. (Eds.). (1999). *Motivating Behavior Change Among Illicit Drug Abusers: Research on Contingency Management.* Washington, DC: American Psychological Association.

Hill, S.Y., DeBellis, M.D., Keshavan, M.S., Lowers, L., Shen, S., Hall, J. & Pitts, T. (2001). Right amygdala volume in adolescent and young adult offspring from families at high risk for developing alcoholism. *Society of Biological Psychiatry, 49,* 894–905.

Hill, S.Y., Lowers, L., Locke, J., Snidman, N., & Kagan, J. (1999). Behavioral inhibition in children from families at high risk for developing alcoholism. *Journal of the American Academy of Child and Adolescent Psychiatry, 38*(4), 410–417.

Hoffman, S.G.. & Tompson, M.C. (Eds.). (2002). *Treating Chronic and Severe Mental Disorders: A Handbook of Empirically Supported Interventions.* New York: Guilford Press.

Hogarty, G.E. (2002). *Personal Therapy for Schizophrenia & Related Disorders: A Guide to Individualized Treatment.* New York: Guilford Press.

Hubbard, R.L. (2005). Evaluation and outcome of treatment. In J.H. Lowinson, P. Ruiz, R.B. Millman, & J.G. Langrod (Eds.), *Substance Abuse: A*

Comprehensive Textbook, 4th ed. Philadelphia: Lippincott Williams & Wilkins, pp. 786–804.

Hurt, R.D., Ebbert, J.O., Hays, J.T., & Dale, L.C. (2003). Pharmacologic interventions for tobacco dependence. In A.W. Graham, T.K. Schultz, & B.B. Wilford (Eds.), *Principles of Addiction Medicine,* 3rd ed. Chevy Chase, MD: American Society of Addiction Medicine, pp. 801–814.

Irvin, J.E., Bowers, C.A., Dunn, M.E., & Wang, M.C. (1999). Efficacy of relapse prevention: a meta-analytic review. *Journal of Consulting and Clinical Psychology, 67*(4), 563–570.

Joe, G.W., Simpson, D.D., & Broome, K.M. (1998). Effects of readiness for drug abuse treatment on client retention and assessment of process. *Addiction, 93*(8), 1177–1190.

Karper, L.P., & Krystal, J.H. (1997). Pharmacotherapy of violent behavior. In D.M. Stoff, J. Breiling, & J.D. Maser (Eds.), *Handbook of Antisocial Behavior.* New York: John Wiley & Sons, Inc., pp. 436–444.

Kemp, A., Kirov, G., Everitt, B., Kayward, P., & David, A. (1998). Randomized controlled trial of compliance therapy. *British Journal of Psychiatry, 172,* 413–419.

Kessler, R.C., Nelson, C.B., McGonagle, K.A., Edlund, M.J., Frank, R.G., & Leaf, P.J. (1996). The epidemiology of co-occurring addictive and mental disorders: implications for prevention and service utilization. *American Journal of Orthopsychiatry, 66,* 17–31.

Koerner, K., & Linehan, M.M. (2000). Research on dialectical behavior therapy for patients with borderline personality disorder. *Psychiatric Clinics of North America, 23*(1), 151–167.

Kosten, T.R., & Sofuoglu, M. (2004). Stimulants. In M. Galanter & H.D. Kleber (Eds.), *Textbook of Substance Abuse Treatment,* 3rd ed. Washington, DC: American Psychiatric Publishing, pp. 189–198.

Kranzler, H.R., & Jaffe, J.H. (2003). Pharmacologic interventions for alcoholism. In A.W. Graham, T.K. Schultz, & B.B. Wilford (Eds.), *Principles of Addiction Medicine,* 3rd ed. Chevy Chase, MD: American Society of Addiction Medicine, pp. 701–720.

Kupfer, D. J., Frank, E., Perel, J. M., et al. (1992). Five-year outcome for maintenance therapies in recurrent depression. *Archives of General Psychiatry, 49,* 769–773.

Leigh, J., Bowen, S., & Marlatt, G.A. (2005). Spirituality, mindfulness, and substance abuse. *Addictive Behaviors, 30*(7), 1335–1341.

Leshner, A.I. (1998). What we know: drug addiction as a brain disease. In A.W. Graham, T.K. Schultz, & B.B. Wilford (Eds.), *Principles of Addiction Medicine,* 2nd ed. Chevy Chase, MD: ASAM, pp. xxix–xxxvi.

Lin, S.W., & Anthenelli, R.M. (2005). Genetic factors in the risk for substance use disorders. In J.H. Lowinson, P. Ruiz, R.B. Millman, & J.G. Langrod (Eds.), *Substance Abuse: A Comprehensive Textbook*, 4th ed. Philadelphia: Lippincott Williams & Wilkins, pp. 33–47.

Linehan, M.M. (1993). *Cognitive-Behavioral Treatment of Borderline Personality Disorder*. New York: Guilford.

Linehan, M.M., Schmidt III, H., Dimeff, L.A., Craft, J.C., Kanter, J., & Comtois, K.A. (1999). Dialectical behavior therapy for patients with borderline personality disorder and drug-dependence. *American Journal on Addictions, 8*, 279–292.

Ling, W., Wesson, D.R., Charuvastra, C., & Klett, C.J. (1996). A controlled trial comparing buprenorphine and methadone maintenance in opioid dependence. *Archives of General Psychiatry, 53*, 401–407.

Livesley, W.J. (Ed.) (2001). *Handbook of Personality Disorders: Theory, Research, and Treatment*. New York: Guilford Press.

Lowinson, J.H., Ruiz, P., Millman, R.B., & Langrod, J.G. (Eds.). (2005). *Substance Abuse: A Comprehensive Textbook*, 4th ed. Philadelphia: Lippincott Williams & Wilkins.

Lyketsos, C.G., Hutton, H., Fishman, M., Schwartz, J., & Treisman, G.J. (1996). Psychiatric comorbidity on entry to an HIV primary care clinic. *AIDS, 10*(9), 1033–1039.

Marcus, M., & Levia, M. (2001). Eating disorders. In D.C. Daley & I.M. Salloum (Eds.), *Clinician's Guide to Mental Illness*. New York: McGraw-Hill.

Marlatt, G.A. (1985). Cognitive assessment and intervention procedures for relapse prevention. In G.A. Marlatt & J. Gordon (Eds.), *Relapse Prevention*. New York: Guildford Press.

Marlatt, G.A. (1996). Taxonomy of high-risk situations for alcohol relapse: evolution and development of a cognitive-behavioral model. *Addiction* 91(Suppl 1), S37–S49.

Marlatt, G.A. (Ed.). (1998). *Harm Reduction: Pragmatic Strategies for Managing High-Risk Behaviors*. New York: Guilford Press.

Marlatt, G.A. (2000). Harm reduction: basic principles and strategies. *Prevention Researcher*, 7, 1–4.

Marlatt, G.A. (2002). Buddhist philosophy and the treatment of addictive behavior. *Cognitive and Behavioral Practice, 9*, 44–49.

Marlatt, G.A., & Donovan, D.M. (Eds.). (2005). *Relapse Prevention: Maintenance Strategies in the Treatment of Addictive Behaviors*, 2nd ed. New York: Guilford Press.

Marlatt, G.A., & Witkiewitz, K. (2002). Harm reduction approaches to alcohol use: health promotion, prevention, and treatment. *Addictive Behaviors, 27,* 867–886.

Martin, C., Earleywine, M., Blackson, T., Vanyukov, M., Moss, H., & Tarter, R. (1994). Aggressivity, inattention, hyperactivity, and impulsivity in boys at high and low risk for substance abuse. *Journal of Abnormal Child Psychology, 22,* 177–203.

McCrady, B., & Epstein, E. (Eds.). (1999). *Addictions: A Comprehensive Guidebook.* New York: Oxford University Press.

McKay, J.R. (1999). Studies of factors of relapse to alcohol, drug, and nicotine use: a critical review of methodologies and findings. *Journal of Studies on Alcohol, 60,* 566–576.

McLellan, A.T. (1985) *Guide to the Addiction Severity Index.* Rockville, MD: NIDA.

McLellan, A.T., Lewis, D.C., O'Brien, C.P., & Kleber, H.D. (2000). Drug dependence, a chronic medical illness: implications for treatment, insurance, and outcomes evaluation. *Journal of the American Medical Association, 284*(13), 1689–1695.

Mee-Lee, D., Shulman, G.D., Fishman, M., Gastfriend, D.R., & Griffith, J.H., (Eds.). (2001). *ASAM Patient Placement Criteria for the Treatment of Substance-Related Disorders* 2nd ed. Chevy Chase, MD: American Society on Addiction Medicine.

Meyer, R.E. (1986). How to understand the relationship between psychopathology and addictive disorders. In R.E. Meyer (Ed.), *Psychopathology and Addictive Disorders.* New York: Guilford, pp. 3–16.

Meyers, R.J., Miller, W.R., Hill, D.E., & Tonigan, J.S. (1999). Community reinforcement and family training (CRAFT). *Journal of Substance Abuse Treatment, 10*(3), 291–308.

Miklowitz, D.J., & Goldstein, M.J. (1997). *Bipolar Disorder: A Family-Focused Treatment Approach.* New York: Guilford Press.

Miller, W.R. (1999). *Integrating Spirituality into Treatment: Resources for Practitioners.* Washington, DC: American Psychological Association (APA).

Miller, W.R., & Rollnick, S. (2002). *Motivational Interviewing: Preparing People to Change Addictive Behavior,* 2nd ed. New York: Guilford.

Minkoff, K., & Drake, R.E. (Eds.). (1991). *Dual Diagnosis of Major Mental Illness and Substance Disorders.* San Francisco: Jossey-Bass.

Monti, P., Adams, D., Kadden, R., Cooney, N., & Abrams, D. (2002). *Treating Alcohol Dependence,* 2nd ed. New York: Guilford.

Montrose, K., & Daley, D.C. (1995). *Celebrating Small Victories: Treating Chronic Mental Illness and Substance Abuse.* Center City, MN: Hazelden.

Moss, H., Vanyukov, M., Majumder, P., Kirisci, L., & Tarter, R. (1995). Per-pubertal sons of substance abusers: influences of parental and familial substance abuse on behavioral disposition, IQ, and school achievement. *Addictive Behaviors, 20,* 1–14.

Mueser, K.T., & Glynn, S.M. (1999). *Behavioral Family Therapy for Psychiatric Disorders,* 2nd ed. Oakland, CA: New Harbinger.

Mueser, K.T., Noordsy, D.L., Drake, R.E., & Fox, L. (2003). *Integrated Treatment for Dual Disorders: A Guide to Effective Practice.* New York: Guilford.

Najavits, L.M., & Weiss, R.D. (1998). "Seeking safety": outcome of a new cognitive-behavioral psychotherapy for women with posttraumatic stress disorder and substance dependence. *Journal of Traumatic Stress, 11,* 437–456.

Narcotics Anonymous (1988). Van Nuys, CA: World Service Office, Inc.

Nathan, P.E., & Gorman, J.M. (Eds.). (2002). *A Guide to Treatments that Work,* 2nd ed. New York: Oxford University Press.

National Institute on Alcohol Abuse and Alcoholism. (1995a). Project Match Series, Volume 1. *Twelve-Step Facilitation Therapy Manual.* Rockville, MD: U.S. Department of Health and Human Services.

National Institute on Alcohol Abuse and Alcoholism. (1995b). Project Match Series, Volume 2. *Motivational Enhancement Therapy Manual.* Rockville, MD: U.S. Department of Health and Human Services.

National Institute on Alcohol Abuse and Alcoholism. (1995c). Project Match Series, Volume 3. *Cognitive-Behavioral Coping Skills Therapy Manual.* Rockville, MD: U.S. Department of Health and Human Services.

National Institute on Alcohol Abuse and Alcoholism. (1999). Update on approaches to alcoholism treatment. *Alcohol Research and Health, 23*(2).

National Institute on Alcohol Abuse and Alcoholism. (2000). *Alcohol and Health: 10th Special Report to Congress.* Rockville, MD: U.S. Department of Health and Human Services.

National Institute on Alcohol Abuse and Alcoholism. (2004). *Combined Behavioral Intervention Manual.* Bethesda, MD: U.S. Department of Health and Human Services.

National Institute on Alcohol Abuse and Alcoholism. (2005). *Helping Patients Who Drink Too Much: A Clinician's Guide.* Rockville, MD: U.S. Department of Health & Human Services.

National Institute on Drug Abuse. (1993). *Cue Extinction.* Rockville, MD: U.S. Department of Health and Human Services.

National Institute on Drug Abuse. (1998a). Therapy Manuals for Drug Addiction, Manual 1. *A Cognitive Behavioral Approach: Treating Cocaine*

Addiction. Rockville, MD: U.S. Department of Health and Human Services.

National Institute on Drug Abuse. (1998b). Therapy Manuals for Drug Addiction, Manual 2. *A Community Reinforcement Plus Vouchers Approach: Treating Cocaine Addiction.* Rockville, MD: U.S. Department of Health and Human Services.

National Institute on Drug Abuse. (1999a). Therapy Manuals for Drug Addiction, Manual 3. *An Individual Drug Counseling Approach to Treat Cocaine Addiction: The Collaborative Cocaine Treatment Study Model.* Rockville, MD: U.S. Department of Health and Human Services.

National Institute on Drug Abuse. (1999b). *Principles of Addiction Treatment: A Research-Based Guide.* Rockville, MD: U.S. Department of Health and Human Services.

National Institute on Drug Abuse. (2000a). *Approaches to Drug Abuse Treatment.* Rockville, MD: U.S. Department of Health and Human Services.

National Institute on Drug Abuse. (2000b). Therapy Manuals for Drug Addiction, Manual 4. *A Group Drug Counseling Approach to Treat Cocaine Addiction: The Collaborative Cocaine Treatment Study Model.* Rockville, MD: U.S. Department of Health and Human Services.

National Institute on Drug Abuse. (2003). Therapy Manuals for Drug Addiction, Manual 5. *Brief Strategic Family Therapy for Adolescent Drug Abuse.* Rockville, MD: U.S. Department of Health and Human Services.

Newman, C.F.L., Beck, A.T., Reilly-Harrington, N.A., & Gyulai, L. (2002). *Bipolar Disorder: A Cognitive Therapy Approach.* Washington, DC: American Psychological Association.

Nowinski, J., & Baker, S. (1998). *The Twelve-Step Facilitation Handbook: A Systematic Approach to Early Recovery from Alcoholism and Addiction.* San Francisco: Jossey-Bass Publishers.

Nunes, E.V., Weissman, M.M., Goldstein, R., et al. (2000). Psychiatric disorders and impairment in the children of opiate addicts: prevalences and distribution by ethnicity. *American Journal on Addictions, 9,* 232–241.

O'Brien, C. (2005). Anticraving medications for relapse prevention: a possible new class of psychoactive medications. *American Journal of Psychiatry, 162*(8), 1423–1431.

O'Brien, C.P., Childress, A.R., Ehrman, R., & Robbins, S.J. (1998). Conditioning factors in drug abuse: can they explain compulsion? *Psychopharmacology, 12,* 15–22.

O'Farrell, T.J., & Fals-Stewart, W. (1999). Treatment models and methods: family models. In B.S. McCrady & E.E. Epstein (Eds.), *Addictions: A Comprehensive Guidebook.* London: Oxford University Press, pp. 287–305.

Onken, L.S., Blaine, J.D., & Boren, J. (1997). *Beyond the Therapeutic Alliance: Keeping the Drug-Dependent Individual in Treatment: NIDA Research Monograph, 165.* Rockville, MD: U.S. Department of Health and Human Services.

Onken, L.S., Blaine, J.D., Genser, S., & Horton, Jr., A.M. (1997). *Treatment of Drug-Dependent Individuals with Comorbid Mental Disorders: NIDA Research Monograph, 172.* Rockville, MD: U.S. Department of Health and Human Services.

Ott, P.J., Tarter, R.E., & Ammerman, R.T. (Eds.). (1999). *Sourcebook on Substance Abuse: Etiology, Epidemiology, Assessment, and Treatment.* Needham Heights, MA: Allyn & Bacon.

Pani, P.P., Maremmani, I., Pirastu, R., Tagliamonte, A., & Luigi-Gessa, G. (2000). Buprenorphine: a controlled clinical trial in the treatment of opioid dependence. *Drug and Alcohol Dependence, 60,* 39–50.

Parran, T.V., Liepman, M.R., & Farkas, K. (2003). The family in addiction. In A.W. Graham, T.K. Schultz, M.F. Mayo-Smith, R.K. Ries, & B.B. Wilford (Eds.), *Principles of Addiction Medicines,* 3rd ed. Chevy Chase, MD: American Society of Addiction Medicine, pp. 395–402.

Payte, J.T., Zweben, J.E., & Martin, J. (2003). Opioid maintenance treatment. In A.W. Graham, T.K. Schultz, M.F. Mayo-Smith, R.K. Ries, & B.B. Wilford (Eds.), *Principles of Addiction Medicines,* 3rd ed. Chevy Chase, MD: American Society of Addiction Medicine, pp. 751–766.

Petry, N.M., & Bickel, W.K. (1999). Therapeutic alliance and psychiatric severity as predictors of completion of treatment for opioid dependence. *Psychiatric Services, 50*(2), 219–227.

Prochaska, J.O. (2003) Enhancing motivation to change. In A.W. Graham, T.K. Schultz, M.F. Mayo-Smith, R.K. Ries, & B.B. Wilford (Eds.), *Principles of Addiction Medicines,* 3rd ed. Chevy Chase, MD: American Society for Addiction Medicine. pp. 825–838.

Prochaska, J.O., & DiClemente, C.C. (1992). Stages of change in the modification of problem behaviors. *Progress in Behavior Modification, 28,* 183–218.

Prochaska, J.O., Norcross, J.C., & DiClemente, C.C. (1994). *Changing for Good.* New York: William Morrow and Company, Inc.

Project MATCH. (1998). Matching alcoholism treatments to client heterogeneity: Project MATCH three-year drinking outcomes. *Alcoholism: Clinical and Experimental Research, 22*(6), 1300–1311.

Rawson, R.A., Obert, J.L., McCann, M.J., & Ling, W. (2005). *The MATRIX Model: Intensive Outpatient Alcohol and Drug Treatment.* Therapist's Manual. Center City, MN: Hazelden.

Roberts, L.J., Shaner, A., & Eckman, T.A. (1999). *Overcoming Addictions: Skills Training for People with Schizophrenia.* New York: W.W. Norton & Company.

Robins, L.N., & Regier, D.A. (1991). *Psychiatric Disorders in America.* New York: The Free Press.

Rosenberg, S.D., Goodman, L.A., Asher, F.C., et al. (2001). Prevalence of HIV, hepatitus B and C in people with severe mental illness. *American Journal of Public Health, 91*(1), 31–36.

Rosenthal, R.N., & Westreich, L. (1999). Treatment of persons with dual diagnosis of substance use disorder and other psychological problems. In B.S. McCrady & E.E. Epstein (Eds.), *Addictions: A Guidebook for Professionals,* pp. 439–476. New York: Oxford University Press.

Ross, H.E., Cutler, M., & Sklar, S.M. (1997). Retention in substance abuse treatment. *American Journal on Addictions, 6*(4), 293–303.

Rounsaville, B.J., Carroll, K.M., & Back, S. (2005). Individual psychotherapy. In J.H. Lowinson, P. Ruiz, R.B. Millman, & J.G. Langrod (Eds.), *Substance Abuse: A Comprehensive Textbook,* 4th ed. Philadelphia: Lippincott Williams & Wilkins, pp. 653–670.

Rounsaville, B.J., & Polin, J. (2000) Substance use disorders measures. In *Handbook of Psychiatric Measures.* Washington, DC: American Psychiatric Association, pp. 457–484.

Rygh, J.L., & Sanderson, W.C. (2004). *Treating Generalized Anxiety Disorder: Evidence-Based Strategies, Tools, and Techniques.* New York: Guilford Press.

Sadock, B.J., & Sadock, V.A. (Eds.). (2000). *Kaplan & Sadock's Comprehensive Textbook of Psychiatry,* 7th ed. Philadelphia: Lippincott Williams & Wilkins.

Salloum, I.M., Daley, D.C., Cornelius, J.R., Kirisci, L., & Thase, M.E. (1996). Disproportionate lethality in psychiatric patients with concurrent alcohol and cocaine abuse. *American Journal of Psychiatry, 153*(7), 953–955.

Salloum, I.M., Daley, D.C., & Thase, M.E. (2000). *Male Depression, Alcoholism, and Violence.* London, UK: Martin Dunitz Ltd.

Salloum, I.M., & Thase, M.E. (2000). Impact of substance abuse on the course and treatment of bipolar disorder. *Bipolar Disorders, 2,* 2269–2280.

Sammons, M.T., & Schmidt, N.B. (Eds.). (2001). *Combined Treatments for Mental Disorders: A Guide to Psychological and Pharmacological Interventions.* Washington, DC: American Psychological Association.

Saxon, A.J. (2003). Special issues in office-based opioid treatment. In A.W. Graham, T.K. Schultz, & B.B. Wilford (Eds.), *Principles of Addiction*

Medicine, 3rd ed. Chevy Chase, MD: American Society on Addiction Medicine, pp. 767–784.

Schmitz, J.M., & Delaune, K.A. (2005). Nicotine. In J.H. Lowinson, P. Ruiz, R.B. Millman & J.G. Langrod (eds.), *Substance Abuse: A Comprehensive Textbook,* 4th ed. Philadelphia: Lippincott Williams & Wilkins, pp. 387–402.

Schuckit, M.A. (2000). *Drug and Alcohol Abuse: A Clinical Guide to Diagnosis and Treatment,* 5th ed. New York: Plenum.

Selzer, M.L. (1971). The Michigan Alcoholism Screening Test: the quest for a new diagnostic instrument. *American Journal of Psychiatry, 127,* 1653–1658.

Seppala, M.D. (2001). *A Clinician's Guide to the Twelve Step Principles.* New York: McGraw-Hill.

Shea, S.C. (1999). *The Practical Art of Suicide Assessment: A Guide for Mental Health Professionals and Substance Abuse Counselors.* New York: John Wiley & Sons, Inc.

Skinner, H.A., (1982). The drug abuse screening test. *Addictive Behaviors, 7,* 363–371.

Soloff, P. (1998). Algorithms for pharmacological treatment of personality dimensions: symptom-specific treatments for cognitive-perceptual, affective, and impulsive-behavioral dysregulation. *Bulletin of the Menninger Clinic, 62*(2), 195–214.

Stanton, M.D. (2004). Getting reluctant substance abusers to engage in treatment/self-help: a review of outcomes and clinical options. *Journal of Marital and Family Therapy, 30*(2), 165–182.

Stanton, M.D., & Heath, A.W. (2005). Family/couples approaches to treatment engagement and therapy. In J.H. Lowinson, P. Ruiz, R.B. Millman, & J.G. Langrod (Eds.), *Substance Abuse: A Comprehensive Textbook,* 4th ed. Philadelphia: Lippincott Williams & Wilkins, pp. 680–689.

Stanton, M.D., & Shadish, W.R. (1997). Outcome, attrition, and family-couples treatments for drug abuse: a meta-analysis and review of the controlled, comparative studies. *Psychological Bulletin, 122*(2), 170–191.

Stein, D.J. (Ed.). (2004). *Clinical Manual of Anxiety Disorders.* Washington, DC: American Psychiatric Publishing, Inc.

Stein, D.J., Kupfer, D.J., & Schatzberg, A.F. (2006). *Textbook of Mood Disorders.* Washington, DC: American Psychiatric Publishing, Inc.

Stine, S.M., Greenwald, M.K., & Kosten, T.R. (2003). Pharmacologic interventions for opioid addiction. In A.W. Graham, T.K. Schultz, & B.B. Wilford (Eds.), *Principles of Addiction Medicine,* 3rd ed. Chevy Chase, MD: American Society on Addiction Medicine, pp. 735–748.

Stoff, D.M., Breiling, J., & Maser, J.D. (Eds.) (1997). *Handbook of Antisocial Behavior.* New York: John Wiley & Sons, Inc.

Swanson, A.J., Pantalon, M.V., & Cohen, R.K. (2002). Motivational interviewing and treatment adherence among psychiatric and dually diagnosed patients. *Journal of Nervous and Mental Disease, 187,* 630–635.

Swartz, M.S., Swanson, J.W., Hiday, V.A., Borum, R., Wagner, H.R., & Burns, B.J. (1998). Violence and severe mental illness: the effects of substance abuse and nonadherence to medication. *American Journal of Psychiatry, 155*(2), 226–231.

Tarter, R. (1990). Evaluation and treatment of adolescent substance abuse: a decision-tree method. *American Journal of Drug and Alcohol Abuse, 16,* 1–46.

Tarter, R., Blackson, T., Brigham, J., Moss, H., & Caprara, G. (1995). The association between childhood irritability and liability to substance use in early adolescence: a two-year follow-up study of boys at risk for substance abuse. *Drug Alcohol Dependence, 39,* 253–261.

Thase, M.E. (1999). Long-term nature of depression. *Journal of Clinical Psychiatry, 60*(Suppl 14), 3–9.

Thomas, J. (2001). Buprenorphine proves effective, expands options for treatment of heroin addiction. *NIDA Notes, 16*(2), 8–11.

Tomasson, K., & Vaglum, P. (1998). Psychiatric co-morbidity and aftercare among alcoholics: a prospective study of a nationwide representative sample. *Addiction, 93*(3), 423–431.

Torrey, E.F. (2001). *Surviving Schizophrenia,* 4th ed. New York: Basic Books.

Torrey, E.F., & Knable, M.B. (2002). *Surviving Manic Depression.* New York: Basic Books.

Triffleman, E., Carroll, K., & Kellogg, S. (1998) Substance dependence and posttraumatic stress disorder therapy. *Journal of Substance Abuse Treatment 17*(1–2), 3–14.

U.S. Department of Health and Human Services (2002). *Report to Congress on the Prevention and Treatment of Co-Occurring Substance Abuse Disorders and Mental Disorders.* Rockville, MD: USDHHS.

U.S. Department of Health and Human Services (2004). *The Health Consequences of Smoking: A Report to the Surgeon General.* Rockville, MD: USDHHS.

Valasquez, M.M., Maurer, G.C., Crouch, C., & DiClemente, C.C. (2001). *Group Treatment of Substance Abuse: A Stages-of-Change Therapy Manual.* New York: Guilford Press.

Vereby, K.G., Meenan, G., & Buchan, B.J. (2005). Diagnostic laboratory: screening for drug abuse. In J.H. Lowinson, P. Ruiz, R.B. Millman, &

J.G. Langrod (Eds.), *Substance Abuse: A Comprehensive Textbook,* 4th ed. Philadelphia: Lippincott Williams & and Wilkins, pp. 564–578.

Verinis, J.S., & Taylor, J. (1994). Increasing alcoholic patients' aftercare attendance. *International Journal of the Addictions, 29* (11), 1487–1494.

Vocci, F.J., Acri, J., & Eklashef, A. (2005). Medication development for addictive disorders: the state of the science. *American Journal of Psychiatry, 162*(8), 1432–1430.

Volkow, N.D., & Fowler, J.S. (2000). Addiction, a disease of compulsion and drive: involvement of the orbitofrontal cortex. *Cerebral Cortex, 10,* 318–325.

Weiss, R.D., & Daley, D.C. (2003). *Understanding Personality Problems and Addiction,* 2nd ed. Center City, MN: Hazelden.

Weissman, M., Markowitz, J.C., & Klerman, G.L. (2000). *Comprehensive Guide to Interpersonal Therapy.* New York: Basic Books.

Westermeyer, J.J., Weiss, R.D., & Ziedonis, D.M. (Eds.). (2003). *Integrated Treatment for Mood and Substance Use Disorders.* Baltimore: Johns Hopkins University Press.

White, B.F., & MacDougall, J.A. (2001). *A Clinician's Guide to Spirituality.* New York: McGraw-Hill.

Wise, R.A. (1998). Drug-activation of brain reward pathways. *Drug and Alcohol Dependence, 51,* 13–22.

Witkiewitz, K., & Marlatt, G.A. (2004). Relapse prevention for alcohol and drug problems: that was Zen, this is Tao. *American Psychologist, 59*(4), 224–235.

Witkiewitz, K., Marlatt, G.A., & Walker, D.D. (2005). Mindfulness-based relapse prevention for alcohol use disorders: the meditative tortoise wins the race. *Journal of Cognitive Psychotherapy, 19,* 221–228.

Ziedonis, D.M., & Trudeau, K. (1997). Motivation to quit using substances among individuals with schizophrenia: implications for a motivation-based treatment. *Schizophrenia Bulletin, 23*(2), 229–238.

Zuckoff, A., & Daley, D.C. (2001). Engagement and adherence issues in treating persons with non-psychosis dual disorders. *Psychiatric Rehabilitation Skills, 5*(1), 131–162.

About the Authors

Dennis C. Daley, Ph.D., is Chief of Addiction Medicine Services and an Associate Professor of Psychiatry at the University of Pittsburgh Medical Center, Department of Psychiatry, at Western Psychiatric Institute and Clinic (WPIC) in Pittsburgh, PA. Dr. Daley has been involved in managing and providing inpatient, partial hospital, and outpatient treatment services for alcohol and drug problems, psychiatric disorders, and co-occurring or dual disorders (substance abuse combined with psychiatric illness) for nearly three decades. He currently oversees a large continuum of over 20 treatment and prevention programs in eight community locations, serving over 8,000 consumers each year. He and his colleagues were one of the first groups in the United States to develop treatment programs for substance use and co-occurring psychiatric disorders.

Dr. Daley has developed several models of treatment for substance use disorders and dual disorders described in treatment manuals. These include *Dual Disorders Recovery Counseling, Group Drug Counseling, Addiction Recovery* and *Relapse Prevention*. He has also developed family programs and educational materials on addiction and dual disorders for families.

Dr. Daley is currently Principal Investigator of the Appalachian Tri-State Node of the National Institute on Drug Abuse's Clinical Trials Network project. He has been or is currently an investigator on ten other NIDA- or NIAAA-funded clinical trials of treatment of addiction or co-occurring disorders. Dr. Daley has been a consultant and trainer on two federally funded research projects at McLean Hospital of Harvard Medical School.

He is Co-Director of the Education Core of the VISN 4 Mental Illness Research, Education and Clinical Care (MIRECC) project, a joint venture between the Pittsburgh and Philadelphia VA Health Care Systems. Dr. Daley is active in teaching and has presented over 400 workshops, lectures, and training seminars in the United States, Canada, and Europe. As a faculty member in the Department of Psychiatry, Dr. Daley provides clinical supervision to residents and provides educational lectures. He also is an Associate Professor at the University of Pittsburgh School of Social Work and previously was a faculty member in the Department of Sociology at Indiana University of Pennsylvania and the Department of Individual and Family Studies of The Pennsylvania State University. Dr. Daley has consulted with numerous social service organizations and has conducted program evaluations throughout the United States and Europe.

Dr. Daley has over 250 publications, including clinician treatment manuals, family and client educational books, workbooks, and videotapes on recovery from alcohol and drug problems, recovery from psychiatric disorders, recovery from dual disorders, and relapse prevention. He was the first professional in the United States to publish interactive workbooks on co-occurring disorders, and one of the first to publish similar materials on recovery from addiction. Dr. Daley's treatment models and recovery materials are used in numerous substance abuse and dual diagnosis treatment programs throughout the United States and other countries.

G. Alan Marlatt, Ph.D., is the Director of the Addictive Behaviors Research Center and Professor of Psychology at the University of Washington. He is renowned for his innovative theoretical and clinical work in the addictions field. Over the past two decades, he has made significant advances in developing programs for both relapse prevention and harm reduction for a range of addictive behaviors.

Dr. Marlatt has made hundreds of presentations at scientific conferences and clinical conferences throughout the world. He has also provided many clinical workshops and consultations to substance abuse treatment agencies.

Dr. Marlatt has published numerous papers, book chapters, books, and client recovery manuals. In addition to co-editing the first editions of *Relapse Prevention: Maintenance Strategies in the Treatment of Addictive Behaviors* (1985) and *Assessment of Addictive Behaviors* (1988), Dr. Marlatt is the editor of *Harm Reduction: Pragmatic Strategies for Managing High-Risk Behaviors* (1998), co-editor of *Changing Addictive Behavior: Bridging Clinical and Public Health Strategies* (1999), and co-author of *Brief*

Alcohol Screening and Intervention for College Students (BASICS): A Harm Reduction Approach (1999). His book *Relapse Prevention* is one of the most extensively cited references in the field of addiction treatment.

He also has written many materials for clients in recovery from an addiction. This includes co-authoring with Dr. Daley the client workbook *Overcoming Your Alcohol or Drug Problem* that accompanies this therapist guide.

Dr. Marlatt is a Fellow of both the American Psychological Association and the American Psychological Society and is a former president of the Association for Advancement of Behavior Therapy. He served as a member of the National Advisory Council on Drug Abuse at the National Institute on Drug Abuse from 1996 to 2002 and served on the National Advisory Council on Alcohol Abuse and Alcoholism Subcommittee on College Drinking from 1998 to 2001. Dr. Marlatt currently holds a Senior Research Scientist Award from the National Institute on Alcohol Abuse and Alcoholism and received the Innovators Combating Substance Abuse Award from the Robert Wood Johnson Foundation in 2001. Previously he was presented with the Jellinek Memorial Award for Alcohol Studies (1990), the Distinguished Scientist Award from the American Psychological Association's Society of Clinical Psychology (2000), the Visionary Award by the Network of Colleges and Universities Committed to the Elimination of Drug and Alcohol Abuse (2002), and the Distinguished Researcher Award from the Research Society on Alcoholism (2004).